C.6 Albany.
London. W. I.

30th November 1962.

Dear Maeve,

I'm sorry I wasn't in when you
telephoned, but only being here for a
few days I'm in a terrible rush.

I'm afraid it's no use my
encouraging you with the idea of film
rights in Titus. It's not a book which
I can imagine lending itself to the films,
and nowadays less than ever. Very few
films are made now except great expensive
epics. I can better imagine a French
director being interested than an English
one and the last of all, I'm afraid, to
be interested would be Carol Reed. It's
completely outside his rather limited sphere
of interest.

I'm very sorry to write so bluntly,
but what are the good of illusions? I'm very
sorry too to hear how ill Mervyn has been.

Yours sincerely,

Graham

Graham Greene thought that *Gormenghast* could not be filmed.
Letter to Maeve Gilmore, Mervyn Peake's wife.

'It was really a question of self-indulgence, the whole book – I enjoy the fantastic.'
Mervyn Peake on BBC radio, 1947

'It is in every way a remarkable work.'
Orson Welles, 1951

'I would not for anything have missed *Gormenghast*. It has the hallmark of a true myth: i.e. you have seen nothing like it before you read the work, but after that you see things like it everywhere.'
C.S. Lewis, 1958

'I'm afraid it's no use my encouraging you with the idea of film rights in Titus. It's not a book which I can imagine lending itself to the films, and nowadays less than ever.'
Graham Greene, 1962

'It is, if you like, a rich wine of fancy chilled by the intellect to just the right temperature ... It is uniquely brilliant, and we are right to call it a modern classic.'
Anthony Burgess, 1968

'It's Dickens on crack.'
John Sessions, 1999

THE ART OF GORMENGHAST

THE MAKING OF A TELEVISION FANTASY

Estelle Daniel

Foreword by
Stephen Fry

With illustrations by
Mervyn Peake

HarperCollinsEntertainment
An Imprint of HarperCollinsPublishers

BBC

HarperCollins*Entertainment*
An Imprint of HarperCollins*Publishers*
77–85 Fulham Palace Road,
Hammersmith, London W6 8JB

www.**fire**and**water**.com

A Paperback Original 2000
9 8 7 6 5 4 3 2 1

A catalogue record for this book
is available from the British Library

ISBN 0 00 257156 0

Typeset in FF Meta
Designed by Tim Harvey

Printed and bound in Great Britain by
Scotprint. Musselburgh

Soundtrack available on Sony Classical.
A BBC video of the serial is also available.

For Katharine, Christian, Rose, Florence, Clover, Tabitha, Eddie, Lewis, Scarlett, Titus and Jack.

The grandchildren of Mervyn Peake.

Contents

'Still Having Too Much Fun'

Stephen Fry

'Can't be done.'

'Impossible.'

'Madness.'

'Are you out of your bloody mind?'

'Oh no. Oh no, no, no, no, *no*. Simply unthinkable.'

'Forget it at once, old onion. It'll never work.'

Just some of the heartening cries of unconditional faith and unbridled optimism that greeted the news that the BBC were going to set about the business of transferring Mervyn Peake's remarkable novels *Gormenghast* and *Titus Groan* to the small (but becomingly wide and richly digital) screen.

Perhaps the first and greatest fight to be fought when trying to foster the belief that Gormenghast has a future on television is the fight to correct misapprehension. Many who have not read the books believe in the three Gs.

Gormenghast is Gothic.

Gormenghast is Gloomy.

Gormenghast is Grotesque.

G for Gothic. It's very hard to know what people mean by Gothic. In architecture it refers to a style of medieval building that involves soaring space and pointy arches and to its eighteenth-century revivalist mode of designer wildernesses and artfully positioned grottoes and ruins. In typescript, Gothic 𝔱𝔢𝔫𝔡𝔰 𝔱𝔬 𝔪𝔢𝔞𝔫 𝔱𝔥𝔦𝔰 𝔨𝔦𝔫𝔡 𝔬𝔣 𝔱𝔥𝔦𝔫𝔤. In literature it applies to romances like Horace Walpole's *Castle of Otranto*, a prototype of the horror writing familiar to cinema-goers today, complete with foolhardy heroines who explore dungeons and peep into coffins at dead of night, a genre exquisitely mocked by Jane Austen in her novel *Northanger Abbey*. From the late 1700s onwards, by way of Mary Shelley, William Beckford and Edgar Allan Poe, a sense of the Gothic continued to titillate and alarm the public until the genre entered our century with Bram Stoker, translated itself into cinema via Nosferatu, Vincent Price and Christopher Lee and

finally fell into the curly-fingernailed clutches of the nightclubbing Goth and maniacal Anne Rice groupie, all black lipstick and corvine locks. In other words Gothic means almost precisely nothing, it is as washed out as the anaemic face of its modern adherent. It certainly has nothing to do with Mervyn Peake, for all that the G-word is as permanently and erroneously affixed to Gormenghast as a horned helmet is tiresomely and wrongly cartooned to the head of a Wagnerian soprano. Gothic attaches to Gormenghast because no one can think of a better description, and how we all love to describe.

If Gothic comes, can Gloom be far behind? It may be that the associations of gloom with Peake come from the word 'Gormenghast' itself and from the family name of its ruling dynasty, Groan. Other character names – Slagg, Swelter and Flay – these too add to the impression that the proper home of Gormenghast and its citizenry is the interior of the agonised throat of Munch's *Scream*. But if there are screams in Gormenghast, they are more likely to be screams of laughter than screams of shredded angst, for Gormenghast, like all the best art, owes more to the comic than to the tragic.

Grotesque, then? Well, yes, here there is an element of truth. But there is a wide world of difference between the Gothic and the comic grotesque. The grotesque in Gormenghast has more in common with Monty Python and Schieler, with Ubu and Gerald Hoffnung, Edmund Gorey, Spike Milligan, Vivian Stanshall and Buñuel, than with gargoyles, shrieks and monsters or the medievalism of Middle Earth.

Peake created a whole world and in order to do so he naturally had to empty it of all the junk that makes up our own. Gormenghast is stripped of any notion of our politics, society, technology, art or history. It therefore, of course, with the paradox of pure fiction, fair whinnies, quivers and neighs with every kind of resemblance to our

world. Freed of denotation, it just reeks of connotation.

Gormenghast is the story of a family, a society, a world that has apparently, when we meet it, always existed. Its inhabitants' lives are as entrenched, constrained and immovably founded as the rocks of the castle itself. Until, that is, a kitchen boy arises from the basement and begins his ascent to power. Everything and everybody young Steerpike comes close to is changed. He brings a terrible kind of freedom to Gormenghast, much as Darwin, Freud, Marx and others brought a terrible freedom to us. But try as one might, it is impossible to see him as all bad. He has appalling ambition, unspeakable cruelty and terrible pride yet for all that there is ruthless glory to him too. There is nothing much to be said, after all, for Gormenghast's ruling family: the unworldly scholasticism of Lord Groan, the indolence and accidie of his wife Gertrude and the romantic sulks of the heir Titus are hilarious, as are the purblind reactionary rituals of protocol minister Barquentine and the affected fussiness of the trusted advisor Prunesquallor. But Steerpike, like all the best villains, has a kind of magnetic glamour all his own, a charm that leads one as reader (and one hopes as

audience too) into the alarming position of accomplice on his murderous trail to the top.

Peake was, as is widely known, an official British artist during the Second World War, one of the very first of the allies to set eyes on the horrors of Belsen. I don't want to suggest that there is an absolute way of reading his books that amounts to an allegorical interpretation, but there is no doubt in my mind that Gormenghast could only have been written in our century. The moral panic and cowardice with which the twentieth century tried to cope with the death of certainty (spiritual, political, social sexual and psychological certainty) has often been written about. An attempt to portray our moral *lethargy* is more seldom attempted. Steerpike, that ever upwardly mobile germ of a young man, is, according to taste, the absolute type of violent revolutionary, socialist intellectual, pitiless bureaucrat, fascist ideologue, fifth columnist, soulless fanatic or criminal sociopath: he is the infection that burrows deep into the apparently impermeable fastness of Gormenghast's bones. The ruling class of Gormenghast and its daft, blundering, eccentric inability to come to terms with Steerpike is the source of the work's most enduring comedy as well as its most biting satire.

When the cast of the BBC's legendary production of *I Claudius* was in rehearsal, anecdote has it that there was a terrific breakthrough for the actors (struggling under togas and the weight of history and Shakespeare) when someone, perhaps the director, perhaps the adapter, pointed out that for all the imperial trappings of the characters, the story was really akin to an epic family saga, not unlike *The Godfather*. Pleasingly (and unknown to the *I Claudius* people), Francis Ford Coppola had helped *his* cast by telling them to forget the mafia and think of the story of *The Godfather* and its Italian Americans as being a modern version of the g(l)ory that was Rome. Gormenghast shares much with those two classic family sagas. The particularities of place, character, title, violence and public turmoil are as nothing to the relationships, family loyalties, betrayals, lusts, ambitions and private torment of its characters. Under the strange names, teeth, costumes, habits and eccentricities of character there are to be found human beings. Human beings, as the saying goes, just like us. The difference is that Gormenghast is positively and proudly non-realist and, much as realist and realistic drama might have its place, the surreal

and the fantastic (I would never call Gormenghast fantasy) have long been underserved on British television.

My connection with the BBC's decision to commit itself to an adaptation of Gormenghast began in the autumn of 1998, when I received a copy of Malcolm McKay's script together with a covering letter from the director, Andy Wilson, asking me to play the schoolmaster, Bellgrove. I thought the script was outstanding and brilliant, as was the covering letter. Without anything other than becoming modesty and a due realisation of the impossibility of what they were attempting, Andy Wilson's letter breathed a spirit, a passion, an intelligence without intellectuality, that made me desperate to be a part of it all.

But against the possibility of Gormenghast ever getting off the ground was set the difficulty of pre-selling such a project around the world in an age when the global pre-sale is all. No one abroad was going to buy such a programme until they'd seen it. But some months after I had seen the script and was still unsure about whether it was going to happen, Alan Yentob and the BBC made the brave decision to commit themselves to the production heart, soul and wallet. I was taken to a Soho lunch with Andy Wilson by the producer, Estelle Daniel, and treated by the pair of them to a marvellous show of drawings, models, photographs, cartoons, postcards and brimming, non-stop enthusiasm. I've never eaten or drunk less at a free lunch in all my life. My mouth was open, but very little passed in or out. The sheer scale of the production was frightening and these two had been living and breathing it for years. They were talking, it seemed to me, about making the equivalent of four British feature films in the time it takes to make one. Dozens of principal roles, for which Estelle and Andy had absurdly ambitious casting plans (which were to be realised), colossal sets housed in five entire sound stages and millions of those achingly rare BBC pounds. What else is a British Broadcasting Corporation for? it might be said. Yet, whatever the fate of this Gormenghast, to have committed to such a thing at a time when the BBC was everybody's favourite target for abuse was a marvellous act of courage, for this was to be no safe costume drama or headline-catching PR coup: Gormenghast is and always will be, *different*, and, like salted orange juice, will never be to everyone's taste.

Once the production was, as they say in America, green-lit, Andy, Estelle and Malcolm,

Mervyn Peake drawing of
Bellgrove and Titus.
*Titus was becoming more
and more difficult to
control ... The professors
found him difficult,
wayward, and on
occasions, insolent. All
except Bellgrove, for
whom Titus had a
fondness and an
inexplicable respect.*
(Gormenghast: ch. 47)

perhaps fortunately, never really had the time to
sit back and absorb what they had committed
themselves to. The BBC wanted the episodes
shown as a Millennial Production and, as
countdown tickers around the world showed, the
year 2000 was approaching with obscene haste.

I was driven to Stage K of Shepperton in
early April for the read-through in the same car
as Christopher Lee, who was to play the butler,
Flay. Such a treat alone was enough to make my
life complete you would think, and you'd be
right. But until you've heard Christopher Lee
singing Wagner, something he did for me in my
dressing room a few weeks later, you haven't
lived. You really haven't.

There was further splendour awaiting. John
Sessions, Celia Imrie, Spike Milligan, Eric Sykes,
Gregor Fisher, Martin Clunes, James Dreyfus, June
Brown, Warren Mitchell, Fiona Shaw, Ian
Richardson, Mark Williams and Richard Griffiths.
Added to them were the startling youthful talents
of Jonathan Rhys Meyers and Andrew Robertson
playing Steerpike and Titus: believe me you will
hear from them again. Good God, what a cast.
The read-through was rendered even more
memorable by a delightful and frankly tear-jerking
speech from Sebastian Peake, one of Mervyn's
sons, who conjured up for us his father's spirit in
a way that none of us present will ever forget.
The constant support and encouragement of the
extended Peake family was one of the many
great pleasures of the whole production. It is not
usual for the relicts of a literary estate to be
anything other than pains in the neck.

Of the principal photography itself and my
own small part in it, I can only say that I have
rarely worked in a more friendly and relaxed
atmosphere. Every day that I came on set I
would ask Andy how he was (I don't think at this
point he had slept for two and a half years – he
certainly hadn't cut his hair for twice that time)
and every day the reply, between puffs of self-
rolled tobacco, was the same: 'It can't be right,
Stephen. I'm still having too much fun.' Andy's
award-winning television achievements on
Cracker and *Psychos* as well as his extraordinary
work devising the suicidal mayhem of Circus
Archaos prepared him better than perhaps
anyone to undertake this task and in Estelle
Daniel he met the perfect match in enthusiasm,
devotion to Peake and weird eccentricity. Estelle
read Scandiwegian languages at university
because she wanted to encounter Ibsen in the
original, which may not argue a very balanced
state of mind but certainly argues an original

one. Her belief in Gormenghast is as unshakeable
as Barquentine's. I left the production, my parts
all in the can, after a month or so of filming. I
have rarely been sorrier to finish a job.

As I write I haven't seen a single frame of
the series. If you are reading this because you
have watched it and want now to dive into the
original, then I know you are in for a grand treat.
Whether or not the filmed version is deemed a
success by critics or by history, Peake's world will
survive our own. At the turn of the next
millennium in a thousand years from now the
Fastness of Gormenghast will eternally be fighting
off the corruption and ambition of Steerpike,
Crow will forever be on Gertrude's shoulders,
Titus will wrestle still with his destiny, Flay will
be locked in endless combat with Swelter and
Professor Bellgrove in clumsy embrace with Irma
Prunesquallor. As Barquentine likes to bark,
kingdoms may come and kingdoms may go, but
Gormenghast remains.

Episode One

'Gormenghast, that is, the main massing of the original stone....' Like a clap of thunder Mervyn Peake's prose poem rolls into being. In a vast castle, an heir is born to the ruling family. The baby, **Titus Groan**, has violet eyes. But the dynasty and its time-honoured rituals are threatened by the charming and evil **Steerpike**, determined to leave his menial position as kitchen boy.

The butler **Flay** and the grotesquely fat chef **Swelter** argue in the kitchens. **Steerpike** makes his bid for freedom, following **Flay** upstairs into the forbidden world beyond.

Titus's mother, **Gertrude**, shows little interest in the baby after he is born, leaving him in the care of the ancient family nursemaid, **Nannie Slagg**. **Gertrude** cares more for cats and birds, particularly an albino rook, **Master Chalk**.

The **Bright Carvers**, who live outside the castle walls, send **Keda** as wet nurse to the infant **Titus**.

Flay locks **Steerpike** in a remote tower. But **Steerpike** escapes across the roofs, ending up in the private quarters of **Fuchsia**, Titus's teenage sister.

Titus is christened in an iron bowl filled with water from the moat, in the first of the rituals that dominate his life.

Steerpike charms **Fuchsia**, appealing to her adolescent fantasy, and soon works his way into a job with the castle physician, **Doctor Prunesquallor**. From this toehold of power, he becomes confidant to Titus's twin aunts, **Clarice** and **Cora**.

He plays on the twins' greed and vanity, and manipulates them into setting fire to the library of **Lord Groan**, the melancholy earl, while the rest of the family are gathered there.

Episode Two

Steerpike assures his place in the castle by stage-managing the rescue of the family from the burning library. They believe he is the hero.

Lord Groan has been driven mad by the loss of his precious books. He sits in the woods, stacking pinecones as if they are books, and tells his daughter, **Fuchsia**, that he is an owl.

Flay is banished by **Gertrude**, after being provoked by **Steerpike** into throwing one of her cats at him.

The wet nurse, **Keda**, tells the baby **Titus** that she will give birth to his sister, then leaves the castle in a thunderstorm.

Amid the first heavy rain, **Swelter** sharpens a kitchen cleaver and makes his way upstairs to settle his argument with **Flay**, before the old retainer leaves.

They fight messily and bloodily through spiders' webs. **Flay** cuts off the chef's ear. **Swelter** flies out through an open window, to die in a puddle in the courtyard.

Lord Groan pulls the corpse up to the top of a tower. He releases a trap-door, and owls swarm over him and the giant body of the chef.

Nobody knows where **Lord Groan** has gone, but **Steerpike** improves his position, first taking command of the search, then being brought in by **Barquentine**, the master of the ritual, to help prepare the 'Earling' ceremony, once **Lord Groan** has been given up for dead.

While the infant **Titus** is 'earled' on a lake, the wet nurse, **Keda**, gives birth to her daughter. In the silence after the ceremony, **Titus** stands and cries out on his raft, answered by the thin cry of the baby, his foster-sister, from the bushes.

Episode Three

Steerpike is now working as apprentice to **Barquentine** in order to learn the castle's innermost secrets. He sets about the seduction of **Fuchsia**, now grown into a woman.

Irma, Doctor Prunesquallor's sister, becomes increasingly frustrated and insists on throwing a party to find herself a husband.

Titus is a schoolboy, educated by a series of eccentric professors. When the old headmaster dies, **Bellgrove** replaces him. His first task is to find **Titus**, who has disappeared on the day of an important ritual.

Titus has escaped through a tunnel. For the first time in his life he is outside the castle walls. He sees a girl who jumps from branch to branch. She is the **Wild Thing**, the girl who has grown up a feral child in the woods, following the death of her mother, **Keda**.

Titus is found by the old retainer, **Flay**, who is living out his exile in a cave. **Flay** reminds him of his lordly duties, and warns him to keep away from the **Wild Thing**, who is not 'of the stones'.

Irma tries to remedy her flat chest on the night of her party by stuffing a hot-water bottle down her ball-gown. She sets her sights on **Bellgrove**, the headmaster, and the two fall instantly in love.

Steerpike poisons **Nannie Slagg**.

Episode Four

Titus, now seventeen, is reminded of his lordly duties by **Gertrude**, but he has no taste for the life of the castle.

Flay returns to the castle to live in secrecy in the deserted east wing. He shadows **Steerpike**, who continues his seduction of **Fuchsia**.

Steerpike kills **Barquentine**, but he is left badly disfigured by burns.

There is a battle of wills between the adolescent and headstrong **Titus**, and the arrogant and confident **Steerpike**. **Titus** confronts him over the onerous rituals which for **Titus** are empty of significance.

In a long-forgotten room, **Flay** and **Titus** find **Steerpike** gloating in madness over the skeletons of **Clarice** and **Cora**, whom he has left to starve to death. **Steerpike** kills **Flay** and makes his escape.

There is a giant thunderstorm, a deluge which floods the whole castle, turning over the social order as the waters rise. **Steerpike** begins a killing spree, using stones fired from a catapult.

Titus runs out through the tunnel, and encounters the **Wild Thing** in a cave, first quietening her, then kissing her. Their lovemaking is interrupted by **Fuchsia**, who runs into the cave to seek shelter from the rain.

The **Wild Thing** runs from the cave and is struck by lightning.

Fuchsia kills herself, drowning in the water.

Titus at last finds courage, and kills **Steerpike**. But, as the rains stop and the flood waters recede, **Titus** turns his back on duty and the empty rituals of the stones, leaving Gormenghast for ever.

Chapter 1

'The Voice of the Pencil'

It all begins and ends in a bookshop. The Saturday before we started shooting *Gormenghast*, I was on Piccadilly with Christopher, who is six, buying a copy of the Gormenghast books for a birthday present. We had been amongst a lot of soothing Water Lilies over the road in the Academy on a mother and son outing. It was to be the last for some months. Our hands were smeared with a Monet palette of pastels and chocolate cake from sketching and eating in the gallery. Bookseller's nightmare.

'Where *is* "Murk and Peep"?' said Christopher, rather graphically, as we trudged up wooden stairs in search of Mervyn Peake. We found him lurking in the Fantasy/Science Fiction section in a suitably New Age cover. Christopher held the book and watched patiently as I moved the remaining volumes on the shelf over to the classics section, and slid them in under 'P' between Orwell and Pepys, a small act of literary

terrorism I learnt from Clare, Mervyn's daughter.

At the cash desk were two male assistants, one check-shirted, knowledgeable, floor-manager type and one twenty-something Soho youth in a greasy black suit. Christopher reached up with the book.

'You don't want to read that, you know. Give you nightmares! I couldn't sleep for a week and I was thirty when I read it!' said Check-shirt. 'No, actually it's one of the greatest books ever written. Did you know they are going to make it into a television serial?'

'Are they really?' I said. Not exactly a lie.

'Oh *no*!' said Greasy Suit. 'They'll make such a balls-up of it. They always do with books.'

'I know,' I said, sympathetically.

'No, no,' said Check-shirt. 'I've seen some of the sets and it looks amazing. Just like the book.' I am the Producer but who was this boy?

'Where was that then?'

Jonathan Rhys Meyers as Steerpike.

opposite: *Steerpike's greedy eyes had devoured the arena ... Everything, he thought to himself, can be of use. Everything.*
(*Titus Groan*: 'A Field of Flagstones')

He blushed. Low voice. '*Radio Times*.' Obviously not the hip item on an Islington coffee table. I remembered a January 1999 pull-out preview for the BBC's Millennial schedule featuring the *Gormenghast* designs. Three months on, and the actors will gather in less than forty-eight hours to read the script together for the first time.

'Yes, I remember something about that now,' I offered. Audience research opportunity. 'I hear they've got that Jonathan Rhys Meyers to play Steerpike.'

'Oh well, in that case,' said Greasy Suit, 'in that case, it might be all right. I'll definitely watch that. Great book.' Christopher is seated at my feet with his back to the oak counter, reading *Gormenghast*, now finger-printed with the violet pastels, rainy-day wellingtons sticking out, guaranteed to trip up anyone else who might want to buy a copy of the book.

'Mum, what is *Gormenghast* about?'

Later, sitting down in great, good company with the cast of *Gormenghast* to seek an answer to this question, I remembered the bookshop. A brief but telling encounter for the producer of the BBC adaptation of the Gormenghast trilogy, mid twentieth-century classic and Millennial drama. So Gormenghast is still read and regarded as a great and disturbing story by the twenty- and thirty-somethings. They will like our sets, I understand, and endorse a Steerpike, who their own generation recognise and want to watch. And there is a move, if only by the producer of the drama and the author's daughter, to shift Gormenghast out of the Fantasy section and back amongst the Classics.

Back in 1994, when the BBC bought the rights to the Gormenghast trilogy, we decided to make the story into a four-part serial to be shown at the Millennium. At that time we were making a raft of frock and carriage classics, *Pride and Prejudice*, *Middlemarch*, a renaissance for the BBC Classic of the eighteenth and nineteenth century. Much loved stories were back on the screen but with a contemporary resonance from a new generation of dramatists and film-makers. Now a move to address the twentieth century, bringing the same approach and production values to those stories. There was no question of making *Gormenghast* before the turn of the century as it struck us all as being the perfect story for then. An ancient world threatened with change, a fading aristocracy, a reluctant prince coming of age versus a villain who seems to embody the history of the century.

In the following five years, we embarked upon a unique development process. During that time we could have made the serial many times over, and sitting with the Cast on a cold March day in Shepperton Studios, poised for production on an epic scale, it was hard to believe that it was all still to come. A cast to die for and a group of creative artists and film-makers with enviable imaginations bringing Peake's world of Gormenghast to the screen for the first time.

When I was asked to produce the piece, I returned to the book. I had read the Penguins as a teenager in a classic edition with the original drawings. Now I found a new edition in the bookshop with a fairy castle on the front. I started to reread Gormenghast to make what I thought might be a difficult decision. I remembered fragments of a strange and compelling story, but felt a faint and irrational mistrust of Gothic castles and dungeons and dragons. This time I read the books in one and failed to recognise the world I first entered at fifteen. I had the same experience with Dickens, reading *David Copperfield* in my teens as a rather long boy's adventure, and coming to it again later as if for the first time, as a towering work about the human condition. Surely the hallmark of the great books, the possibility of finding complete worlds within them that echo each of the phases of a lifetime. It was the second reading of Peake that formed the vision of Gormenghast I have sought to bring to the screen.

I saw this world the second time through the eye of a painter. I like Peake's phrase, 'the voice of the pencil'. A palette of carefully chosen colours, sculptural textures, scale, lighting – it seemed like a great canvas from a twentieth-century artist. At fifteen I had barely looked at painting. Now with adult knowledge of the work of Picasso, Miro and Klee, as I read, I saw something else. The art of Gormenghast. There was none of the heart-warming nostalgia for an old-fashioned world I associate with the kingdoms of Tolkien. There were no dungeons or dragons. In fact there is no magic in Gormenghast at all.

I understood how this visual world could be the backdrop for a film, the perfect medium for Mervyn Peake, artist and storyteller at the same time. In amongst the painterly descriptions, it is easy to cut to the plot, as one does reading it young. A story with classical, Shakespearean dimensions but the pace and event of the best thrillers. Six murders, three tragic deaths and two

The Groan household. Back row from left: Warren Mitchell as Barquentine, June Brown as Nannie Slagg, Fiona Shaw as Irma Prunesquallor, John Sessions as Dr Prunesquallor, Christopher Lee as Flay, Zoë Wanamaker as Clarice, Lynsey Baxter as Cora. Front row from left: Celia Imrie as Gertrude, Ian Richardson as Lord Groan, Neve McIntosh as Fuchsia.

seductions. It struck me as wildly comic and terribly frightening all at once.

Then there were the people of Gormenghast. Like the story, they seemed to be classical, satirical yet contemporary. I found Lear and Cordelia in Lord Groan and Fuchsia, or was it Ophelia? The royal antics present a parody of the English aristocracy. Titus seemed a kind of Hamlet in essence, whilst Steerpike was both the voice of the century, the fascist dictator, and the face of the future. In him I also recognised the meddler with Fate, the ultimate practical joker – 'What if I play this trick, what if I fiddle with the way of things?' It is a high-powered game of dice, the source of much extraordinary fiction.

I had entered the castle, it seemed. The preparations for the programme followed and took some years to complete to our satisfaction. It was a shared vision, nurtured by myself and Andy Wilson, the director. Andy and I had collaborated on two films and enjoy a kind of easy synchronicity in the areas of art and comedy, which is a constant pleasure. The foundation stone was a great script from Malcolm McKay, turned with great pace, wit and invention. I regard Malcolm as one of the best contemporary dramatists. He possesses, to borrow an expression of Peake's, 'the kind of authority that moves against time for a few feverish seasons'. We then set about answering the BBC's biggest question, 'Where is Gormenghast?' To this they added, 'Who are they?' and 'How much?' We added, in the words of Steerpike, 'What's it all for?'

The 'who' question seemed to answer itself. From early on we received approaches from some of the great British stars of film and comedy, a rare situation in which to find oneself. And of those we approached, many were long-term fans of the book. Christopher Lee knew Mervyn Peake. The 'how much' question was answered by an intensive and unusual period of work on the part of director, designer and producer. The world was designed, the director drew out storyboards, like cartoons, of all the action and we planned all the computer effects one by one. We specified exactly what we needed to see, and did numerous sums – to work out the price of a World.

There then followed a summer in the States talking to co-producers about *Gormenghast*. We encountered then as never before the difficulty in describing it. Gormenghast isn't on the map and nobody had been on holiday there. We sat in chilled offices in LA with American TV executives,

amidst Merlin paraphernalia, recently transmitted over there and, it seemed, an example to us all. They had sold videos on air off the back of the programme like hot potatoes. The cast was quoted as ground-breaking: 'Sam Neill, Isabella Rossellini, Rutger Hauer, Miranda Richardson, John Gielgud, Helena Bonham Carter.' They told us, 'It proves you can make a great mini-series without big stars!!' We pitched and played with words: 'Think *Blackadder*, think *Six Wives of Henry the Eighth*. *Gormenghast* is all this and much more. *Monty Python* crossed with the Royal Family?' 'But could it be called Liverpool?' they said. 'We've heard of that!' And 'Could Lord Groan come back as a ghost, like in *Hamlet*?'

Back in London, we persuaded the BBC we had the answer to the big question 'Where is Gormenghast?' We showed them drawings and models on a grand scale and they said, 'Now we see. The best kind of BBC Classic. James Cameron vision cut for BBC cloth!' We had designed the whole thing for Pinewood studios as it had always been clear we must make this world ourselves, with the best artists we could find. We had looked at film of castles from Edinburgh to Jaipur and there had been constant requests to make it on location or in Prague, so it could be more easily realised and afforded, perhaps more familiar. But on this we had stood our ground.

This formed the starting point of my own vision. Gormenghast must be a hand-made place, and one of immense beauty. We must see that, although the ritual is cumbersome and repellent to Titus, his surroundings are exquisite. Thus he is caught in the pull of an awesome current, back towards the castle, whilst his instincts pull him forward to freedom and away. In his book *A Child of Bliss*, Sebastian, Mervyn Peake's son, describes coming of age and leaving the Peake household. The image he uses became my touchstone.

'On leaving home I left the oil and pencils, the pine table and the green covered Georgian chairs ... I left the smell of something dear, precious, untranslatable. A mystery, something to die for, to kill for, to protect, to cherish, to which to remain fearlessly loyal, to revere and be proud of, something which was irreplaceable. At the end of *Gormenghast*, although he is physically walking away, Titus is, I think, walking forwards and backwards at the same time. Away from his home, the castle, his mother the countess; but back to them at the same time. I think of a ship in a great storm that is further back than when the storm broke despite seeming to go forward, for the power of the elements is pulling it back.'

Her hair, a very dark red colour of great lustre ... Here, if anywhere, was the nest of nests, softer than moss, inviolate, and warm. (Titus Groan: 'The Burning')

THE COUNTESS OF GROAN

21 'The Voice of the Pencil'

Along the way we have constantly been confronted with the notion that Gormenghast is a fundamentally unsympathetic world, peopled by unappealing characters. I have been puzzled and fascinated by this. Like Dickens, it seems to me that the characters, although extreme and grotesque in some senses, are fundamentally sympathetic and viewed with warmth and humour by Peake. Still it has been this abiding notion of the beauty of the world created by the artist that has informed our thoughts on this. Early on we visited Fabian, Mervyn's other son, to see the original drawings of the characters. They are extraordinarily fine and delicate. What struck us most was the gentle softness to the 'voice of the pencil'. We had imagined Lady Groan as something of a hard-edged, ugly old battleaxe. In Fabian's front room we saw a soft drawing of an immense, voluptuous and intensely feminine woman, long curls playing round her face and small delicate birds caught in the tresses. We have built the characters and their costumes up, then, from a softer base than we had originally anticipated. This was understood by Johnny Rhys Meyers right from the outset. Later, as he developed the character, I was fascinated hearing him talk about Steerpike and ideas of love. If,

when Steerpike was caught by Flay in the Stone Lanes, right at the beginning, Flay had taken him in and given him love, it would all have been different, he says. Words of compassion to underpin a study of corruption.

Who are they, where is it – and 'what's it all for?' The artists of the twentieth century sought to create their own worlds. Picasso, Max Ernst and Matisse created worlds that echoed this world but were essentially worlds of their own imagination, characterised by a strong individual voice and an unmistakable unique mark. Mervyn Peake wrote his world down, but with the vision of the twentieth-century painter. C.S. Lewis wrote to him, while reading *Gormenghast*, understanding the originality and the nature of this created world, 'I would not for anything have missed *Gormenghast* ... It has the hallmark of a true myth: i.e. You have seen nothing like it before you read the work, but after that you see things like it everywhere.'

As the production gathered momentum through the autumn of 1998, we had recreated this world and partly peopled it. I had come to see Mervyn Peake as a man with an imagination like a castle with countless rooms. Peake the poet, the writer, the painter, the illustrator ... a talent so diverse that it seemed to have been a complicated job for both himself and those that followed to harness it. The persistent difficulty of describing things, of pinning them down. The vision for the production had grown as we had discovered these rooms one by one and entered them, and given them form and substance. It is in the unravelling of this imagination and its history that we have tried to ground *Gormenghast*.

As autumn turned to winter we were poised for production, a great party of us by now. But the deadline to start our run-up to filming came and went and we lost our studio booking at Pinewood to James Bond, plus a handful of our key personnel. Most stayed, and I worried as I watched them doggedly turn down other work that the world of Groan might after all be a dream on a mountain top. But then, with an immense push from several corners of the BBC and a large leap of faith, we made the figures add up and received a call from Alan Yentob to tell us we were in business, three weeks late but still on target for the Millennium. I phoned the Peake family with the news. Titus Groan was to be born. It was the seventeenth of November 1998, and the thirtieth anniversary of the death of Mervyn Peake.

Dear Sir

May I make so free as to tell you what a profound impression your *Titus Groan* and *Gormenghast* are making on me? 'Are making', because, thank goodness, I have not yet finished the second ... I suppose they must have been talked about a good deal (they wouldn't otherwise have reached me who, for all I know what's going on, might as well be always asleep among the Bright Images) but I am sure they are not rated at their true worth. People now all seem to want a 'slice of life' ... or a 'comment on life'. To me those who merely comment on experience seem far less valuable than those who *add* to it, who make me experience what I never experienced before. I would not for anything have missed *Gormenghast*. It has the hallmark of a true myth: i.e. you have seen nothing like it before you read the work, but after that you see things like it everywhere ... That is why fools have (I bet) tried to 'interpret' it as an allegory. They see one of the innumerable 'meanings' which are always coming out of it (because it's alive and fertile) and conclude that you begun – and ended – by *putting* in that, and no more.

If they tell you it's too leisurely and the story takes a long time to develop, don't listen to them. It ought to be, and must be, slow. That endless, tragi-farcical, unnecessary, ineluctable sorrow can't be abridged. I love the length; I like things long – drinks, love-passages, walls, conversations, silences, and above all books ...

Thank you for adding to a class of literature in which the attempts are few and the successes very few indeed.

Yours truly
C.S. Lewis

MAGDALENE COLLEGE,
CAMBRIDGE.

10 / 2 / 58

Chapter 2

War Artist

Gormenghast is a product of the Second World War. While the world was tearing itself apart with a savagery which would leave fifty million dead, Mervyn Peake was moving around England on futile training manoeuvres, and all the time he was writing. He had tried to keep himself out of the forces, not because he was a pacifist or rebel, but because he saw it as a waste of his talents. Artist friends, including Sir Kenneth Clark, Augustus John and Epstein wrote to the War Office to press his case to be employed as a war artist, but their attempts failed. So Gunner Peake 5917577 was called up, and his long flowing black hair was cut off – his army number was to appear in *Gormenghast*, as part of the impossibly long number of an edict which is read to the schoolmasters. At the end of his first leave from the army, in the spring of 1940, he left his wife

with the first handwritten instalment of the epic which would be *Titus Groan*, the first book in the Gormenghast trilogy.

He wrote in 'publishers' dummies', throughout the war. They were blank hardback books, and he would write on them, or on any piece of paper he could find, sticking the additions into the 'dummies'. At the end of each home leave, they would pile up under the bed, as *Titus Groan* came to life. His wife Maeve kept them with her all the time, even sleeping with them, so that she could move them quickly in case of an air raid.

For part of the time they were together, in married quarters in Blackpool, living above an RAF man who played Glenn Miller, while Mervyn wrote and wrote. *In the Mood* and *Moonlight Serenade* downstairs, while upstairs the fantastic world of Gormenghast was being created in the publisher's virgin dummies. Maeve remembered: 'I still cannot read passages of his book without it awakening in me the sweet nostalgia of evenings which belonged to a nether world of waiting, a world that we all knew one day would end, and a world which hung suspended.'

But for most of the time they were apart, Mervyn moving round the dismal England of the war, while Maeve lived in rented cottages in Sussex. Their first son, Sebastian, was born there in 1940, and for him the landscape of Gormenghast is the landscape of his Sussex childhood, the castle is the looming castle of Arundel, on its steep hill above the town, and the Gormenghast lake is the reed-fringed lake below.

Despite the distractions of army life, Mervyn Peake had poems published in the *Listener*, the *Spectator* and the *London Mercury*. He illustrated a book, *Witchcraft in England*, and a book of nursery rhymes, *Ride a Cock-Horse*. The poet Walter de la Mare, who was by then a friend, described them as touching and profound, but also grotesque, and genuinely sinister: 'How

Mervyn Peake in Sussex, where he began to write *Titus Groan*.

opposite: Mervyn Peake in his brief summer as a war artist in 1945. Augustus John compared him to Goya in his treatment of wartime subjects.

The title page in Mervyn Peake's first draft, with an early macabre spelling of the castle name.

Illustration for *Ride a Cock-Horse and other Nursery Rhymes.* 'I had a little husband No bigger than my thumb ...'

Anyhow, most other illustrated books for children look just silly by comparison.'

In the folklore which any family carries around as baggage, its shared memory, the Peake family tell a story of Mervyn being locked out of a shelter in an air raid on the Isle of Sheppey without his helmet. And another more macabre memory is of a room he stayed in with a stain on the ceiling. When he asked what the stain was, he was told it was the mark left when a former occupant had shot himself in the head.

In 1942, soon after the birth of his second son, Fabian, Mervyn Peake had a nervous breakdown. It does not seem to have been one particular event which pushed him over the edge of sanity, more the accumulation of petty demands made on him as a soldier, which came into such profound conflict with his vivid and vibrant imagination.

After he had the breakdown, Mervyn wrote to his closest friend, Gordon Smith, 'I bent down to do up my boot-lace, when I suddenly realised that I could never obey another order again, not ever in my whole life.'

Gordon Smith believed that the absurd life of ritual imposed on the inhabitants of Gormenghast was inspired by the useless years which Mervyn spent in the army. The rituals do not give the Groan family any comfort or satisfaction, but are tedious drills to be got through. Ancient truths which must once have had profound significance to the inhabitants have degenerated into high comedy.

In another bitter letter Mervyn wrote to Gordon Smith, 'I'm sick, sick, sick of it – the perpetual littleness of the life – the monotonous conversation of what I suppose are my comrades who are with me polishing the buttons and blancoing the webbing in our fight against world tyranny.'

Early in the war, when he admitted that he could drive, Mervyn had been posted to teach soldiers how to drive heavy vehicles, which he had no idea about. In the interim, he believed he had learnt nothing of any use. At one point he was posted to Salisbury Plain, for a course in 'theodolites'.

He did not know what they were, even after his first lecture, and he appealed to his commanding officer to be allowed to sit at the back of the room and write his book. Maeve recalled, 'He spoke a little of *Titus Groan*, and the commanding officer, who had been puffing at a pipe, removed it, cleaned out the bowl carefully with a pipe-cleaner, and then tapped it gently on

many nurseries you may have appalled is another matter. How many scandalised parents may have written to you, possibly enclosing doctors' and neurologists' bills, you will probably not disclose.

his right hand. There was a positive sound of wood hitting wood. It *was* a sound of wood hitting wood, for his right hand was a wooden hand. He told Mervyn that … he might continue to write his book.'

Finally the army decided that he was not contributing to the war effort, and he was invalided out. He and Maeve lived for a while in a cottage at the bottom of the garden of his father's house in Sussex, and it was here that *Titus Groan* was completed.

It was only later, after the Germans had surrendered, that Mervyn Peake achieved the ambition he had set himself six years before, to make drawings chronicling the madness which had engulfed Europe. He was commissioned as a war artist to go to Germany.

Augustus John had encouraged him throughout the war, complaining to him, in a letter in 1942, that too many drawings which

emerged from the war were on the 'comic side of warfare' – cartoons to keep up morale. He wrote, 'You, like Goya, are interested rather in its serious side.'

Mervyn Peake ended up at Belsen, soon after the concentration camp had been liberated by the allies. Its inmates continued to die of malnutrition and disease even after the Germans were pushed back.

Haunting drawings flowed from this trip: a plump woman warder (who spat in his face after he did the picture), a condemned Nazi war criminal sitting primly in a bare cell, with his hat on a hook, and compelling, terrible images of a young girl dying in a hospital bed.

The twenty-four hours Mervyn Peake spent in Belsen were to change his life.

Gordon Smith, who apart from being his closest friend, had a professional interest in this, since he had a doctorate for work on the psychology of creative imagination, wrote tellingly that Belsen 'left a deepening wound' on Mervyn Peake.

He suffered from the sensitivity of a man observing horror with the eye of a professional, at the same time fearing that he is a voyeur. The helpless shame of the artist, who is unable to do anything but record events, while gaining inspiration from this most profound suffering, gnawed at him. And the concentration camp echoes across the Gormenghast books.

Mervyn Peake's eldest son has spent a large part of his adult life visiting concentration camps

Belsen 1945

If seeing her an hour before her last
Weak cough into all blackness I could yet
Be held by chalk-white walls, and by the great
Ash coloured bed,
And the pillows hardly creased
By the lightness of her little jerking head –
If such can be a painter's ecstasy,
(Her limbs like pipes, her head a porcelain skull)
Then where is mercy?
And what irony?
Is this my calling, for my schooled eyes see
The ghost of a great painting, line and hue
In this doomed girl of tallow?
O anguish! has the world so white a yellow
As the pernicious and transparent mist
That like a whiff of Belsen in her cheeks
Detaches her by but a breath from linen …

'The Consumptive: Belsen 1945' from *The Glassblowers*.

and reading about the Holocaust, wondering all the time about the effect on his father. Sebastian wrote that the experience 'remained in his conscious and subconscious mind until he died ... he suffered and later died as a result of seeing manifest the antithesis of joy, love and beauty. How can his experience of the camp not have created an eternal helplessness of the soul?'

Titus Groan was published in 1946.

The publication followed a chance meeting early in the war with Graham Greene at the Café Royal in Regent Street. Maeve wrote, 'We went on the first night in London to the Café Royal, where we knew an infinite number of people ... Red plush couches and marble tables, and an evening spent if need be with just one cup of coffee. The elixir came from the lively minds of so many people now dead.'

Graham Greene asked Mervyn that night what he was writing, and he followed up the conversation a couple of years later when he was working with Eyre and Spottiswoode, although when he first saw the manuscript he was brutal. He wrote from the Reform Club in 1945, 'I'm going to be mercilessly frank – I am very disappointed in a lot of it & frequently wanted to wring your neck because it seemed to me you were spoiling a first-class book by laziness ... I began to despair of the book altogether, until

suddenly in the last third you pulled yourself together and ended splendidly ... I want to publish it; but I shall be quite sympathetic if you say "to hell with you" ... If you want to call me out, call me out – but I suggest we have our duel over whisky glasses in a bar.' The book was substantially revised, and Greene did publish it! Coming from such unpromising origins as the damp barracks of wartime England, *Titus Groan* is an extraordinary feat of the imagination. The roots of the book lie in Mervyn Peake's childhood in China.

He was born in 1911, in a bungalow in the hills in Kuling, above the Yangtse River, where his family retreated from the heat for the summer. To the Chinese, the missionaries and businessmen and diplomats were 'foreign devils', and they lived apart. Mervyn Peake's children believe that this upbringing was hugely influential in their father's work. Sebastian says, 'China is there the whole time, underlying the edifice of Gormenghast.' This world of a privileged elite within diplomatic walls, surrounded by the teeming mass of China, may have been the first model for the division between those who live inside Gormenghast castle, and those who live outside in **'those mean dwellings that swarmed like an epidemic around its outer walls. They sprawled over the sloping earth, each one half way over its neighbour until, held back by the castle ramparts, the innermost of these hovels laid hold on the great walls, clamping themselves thereto like limpets to a rock.'** (*Titus Groan*)

The description is clearly of Asian mud huts, not of anything which could be seen in Britain by the twentieth century. China never let Mervyn go. Maeve told his first biographer, John Watney: 'I don't think he ever intended Titus to return to Gormenghast, just as he ... could never see himself returning to China. But, just as he retained always a memory of his distant childhood in China, so Titus would always have kept with him the memory of his childhood at Gormenghast.'

As a child, Mervyn's mind was filled with sites like the road to Peking, which was flanked by giant carvings, his horizon a range of mountains of a kind unknown in Britain. And there is another key element in Gormenghast which must have come from China: the overpowering complexity of the ritual (even if it took the meaningless drudgery of army life to bring this inspiration to full flower). Mervyn was born as the old order was changing. The infant Emperor, heir to the 300-year-old Manchu

The road to Peking. Photo taken by Dr Earnest Cromwell Peake.
Sculpture whose bright files surged over the dust in narrowing perspective like the highway for an emperor.
(*Titus Groan*: 'The Hall of the Bright Carvings')

dynasty, was overthrown in a revolution in July 1911, the month that Mervyn was born, and his father went down from the hill-station to help the Red Cross in Hankow, where there was fierce fighting. It was not safe for the family to come

The hill-station resort Kuling, China. Mervyn Peake's birthplace.

Dr Peake's missionary hospital in Tientsin.

down from the mountains until the end of the year, and then they moved to a hospital closer to the capital Peking, on a dry cold Asian plain.

China was dividing into different spheres of influence, not to be united fully again until Mao's communist take-over after the whirlwind of the Second World War. Sebastian Peake believes that the Chinese response to their problems registered strongly with his father. The Chinese sought comfort in historical context, in ordering and numbering things. Sebastian says, 'There was a historical numerical order, that for example things had to be performed in the tenth month after the previous emperor had died, for the sustaining of the momentum of the historical progress of China. These rituals were very much part of the upper-class Chinese imperative, to seek discipline and order within historical facts.' There is something of the denseness of the ritual of Gormenghast in this memory.

Mervyn Peake once began notes for an autobiography which he never completed. Chapter 1 was to begin: 'Box within box like a Chinese puzzle – so it seems to me, was my childhood. Only half do I believe in those far-away days, lost in the black and engulfing sea.' The growing imagination of this sensitive boy must have found its fuel in places like Kublai Khan's Forbidden City, itself cloaked inside two other cities in a box which was four miles long in

Peking, where the Jade Carvers had their own place among the other castes and classes among the maze of walls. Surely they became the 'Bright Carvers', whose art is at the centre of the ritual in Gormenghast.

Now, at the turn of the Millennium, those days early in the century seem a distant and vanished culture. China was not of course part of the British Empire, but it was on the map of the Empire-builders, men of immense spiritual and cultural hubris, whose vanity over-reached the areas on the map which were already painted red to the lands beyond. British merchants and bankers held the ring in Hong Kong and Shanghai, and shared out huge territories in the South China Seas with other European powers, while in the interior of China, British missionaries like Dr Peake took their message.

The way English children were brought up in those colonial days gave them an access to the undercurrents of their society which sometimes their parents may not have had. The children of the missionaries were learning about China from their nannies and gardeners and cleaners, while their fathers were teaching, saving souls, or in Dr Peake's case, sawing off limbs (witnessed once by the young Mervyn, who crept up to an unguarded window of the surgery. He said later, 'I didn't mind till the thing was off, when they put it on a tray and dumped it by the window, right underneath me. Then I keeled over.')

He rode to school on a donkey, and

developed a comedy routine with a traffic policeman on a junction which he passed every day. The English schoolboy would reach out and knock off the policeman's hat as he passed.

His father had a scientific interest which went into many different areas. Among the Peake family's possessions to this day are a gall stone the size of a cricket ball which Dr Peake removed from the stomach of a Chinese woman patient, and a set of photographs of public executions. Some show the head in mid-air the moment after it was severed.

When he was twelve, the family left China, and Mervyn went to board at Eltham School in what is now south London, but was then in open countryside. On his only other trip to England, when he was very young, a journey from China which took twelve days on the train, his brother was almost left behind in the wilderness in Siberia. The train had stopped in the middle of nowhere to take on water, and Leslie Peake got out to watch an engineer tapping the wheels. The train had begun to move before anyone realised that he was still outside in the snow. His father just got an arm to him in time to pull him in.

Eltham School, which had a policy of catering for the sons of missionaries, makes a very clear appearance in *Gormenghast*. The game that the boys play (which ends up in the death of the headmaster De'ath, Spike Milligan) was once played at Eltham. The giant London plane tree, close to a classroom window, which they used to swing around after slipping along on a specially polished board, is still there. The teachers are modelled on his teachers. Gordon Smith, who was also at the school, recognised it immediately. He wrote, 'The Master's Common Room, a shabby

right: The first Bright
Carving? Mervyn Peake as
an art student in the
garden of the Wallington
house 1932.

far right: Mervyn Peake
with Miss Renouf, his first
landlady on Sark.
*On her shoulders sat a
stonechat, and a huge
raven which was asleep.
The bed-rail boasted two
starlings, a missel-thrush
and a small owl.*
(*Titus Groan*: 'Tallow and
Birdseed')

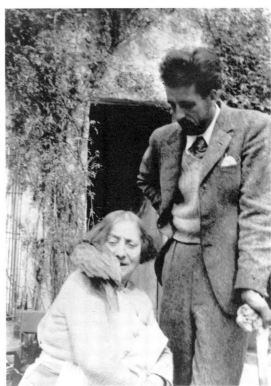

and inadequate place down the passage from the Central Hall, reappears in one of the Gormenghast books as he used to glimpse it, skating past the half-open door: the petty squabbles, the anthracite fire, and the rows of shiny greenish gowns hanging from the wall.'

According to Smith, Mervyn Peake was well liked at school 'for his extravagant sense of humour, the general air of piratical gusto he exuded, his notoriety as an artist, and, no doubt, because he was a sympathetic and likeable person.' As a teenager Mervyn could recite *Treasure Island* by heart, claiming to be able to pick it up from any line in the book, and he was an enthusiastic sportsman, a demon on the rugby field.

He went from school to art college, first to the Croydon School of Art, and then to the Royal Academy Schools. But he never settled into the academic discipline, and two years into his course, although he was winning prizes and selling paintings, he answered a call from a former Eltham teacher, Eric Drake, who had set up an artists' colony on Sark.

Mervyn lived and worked on Sark for two years. His book *Mr Pye* (recently republished) is set specifically on the island, but the inspiration of Sark did not stop there. It informed and infused much of his other art and writing. Gordon Smith wrote that, 'The island became, one way and another, very much part of his mythological landscape.'

Pictures of him there show a strikingly good-looking young artist, with dark hair and deep deep dark eyes, posing for the camera in front of his easel. On this strange leftover Norman possession, there are still old people who remember the young Peake. They speak of him as an eccentric, one of a group of bohemians whose ways were not the ways of the Sarkese. He kept pet cormorants, another skill he learned in his Chinese childhood, where they train cormorants to catch fish, tying a string around their necks to prevent them from swallowing the fish. One Sark resident threatened to sue him because when he appeared in a painting he was made to 'look like a monkey!' Another Sarkese man was punched by Mervyn in the pub for criticising the artists' clothing as 'effeminate'. The fight did not make Mervyn an enemy; on the contrary, it led to an invitation to play in goal for Sark against Guernsey!

When he first came to Sark, Mervyn lived in a small tin hut, painting and writing all the time. Later he lodged with an old woman called Miss Renouf, who kept tame birds, among them a white bird which would sit on her shoulder, surely the model for the white rook who accompanies Lady Groan everywhere in Gormenghast.

Sark is tiny, a universe not more than three and a half miles long, and just a mile and a half wide at its widest point. It is Europe's last feudal stronghold ruled still by the 'Seigneur'. And it is

'For a time the young man lived in a barn that leaked. He worked in the potato fields to make enough money to buy food, he fished in the sea, he washed his own clothes, and did many "inartistic" jobs, and he says it is glorious.'
Daily Herald, 2 May 1934

Portrait of the artist ...

secretive. High cliffs disguise the entrance harbour, which can be reached only by a tunnel carved into the rock. Mervyn Peake came to know the island as well as anyone did, scrambling down steep rock faces with a cormorant in his pocket to explore the dozens of small bays and beaches. Once he found the carcass of a whale, rotting on a beach. He cut out three of its giant vertebrae, and he wrote about them and painted them for years, keeping them in his studios.

The Sark painters were briefly fashionable, with an exhibition in London every year that Mervyn was there. His first known review was by a writer from the *Guernsey Press*, who described him as 'a young man still on the sunny side of twenty-two whose versatility and imagination place him in a class of his own'.

By 1935, Mervyn's paintings had attracted the attention of the Westminster School of Art, where he was invited to become a teacher, and he moved back from Sark. A year later, he met Maeve Gilmore, on her first day as an art student. In her remarkable and unsentimental memoir of their life together, *A World Away*, Maeve recalled her halting first conversation with him in a sculpture class. She had asked him what he painted, and he had replied, 'I'd paint a dustbin if I thought it beautiful.' It was such a strange comment that it overcame the natural shyness of a nineteen-year-old just out of

convent school. He was living in a studio above a warehouse in Hester Road across the river in then unfashionable working-class Battersea. She made her first trip there in a car driven by her mother's chauffeur, Penfold, 'who waited patiently outside for several hours, until I stepped down the stairs, another girl in another clime, never to return to what I thought I knew'.

Mervyn Peake drawing of
Maeve Gilmore with their
first son Sebastian.

For the young upper-class girl, the journey to Battersea (which soon she was doing without a chauffeur!) became like the passage to an enchanted world. To her, it was like going into Fuchsia's attic, a place of mystery and delight. Once she felt the earth was moving, and it really was: an elephant from a circus was being housed for the night in the warehouse below, and as it paced around, the whole floor moved, so precarious was its construction!

Maeve's family were suspicious of the dark-haired artist their daughter had brought home. They sent her to Europe for six months 'to get over it', but Mervyn was waiting for her at Victoria station on her return after writing to her every day, and her family bowed to the inevitable. They had a Catholic marriage, with Mervyn's nonconformist missionary parents making all the compromises.

When Maeve spent her time in exile from Mervyn, she lived in a castle on the Rhine. She saw Hitler at a rally in Nuremberg, and later remembered her host collecting pieces of silver paper for munitions for the 'next war'. Hitler's march into Czechoslovakia in 1938 came on the day of the first major solo exhibition of Mervyn Peake's drawings, in a gallery in St James's. By then he was illustrating regularly in the *London Mercury* as well as taking commissions for portraits. But it was the pictures of ordinary people which seem to have inspired him most:

people he would see on the train, tramps asleep on the embankment, a match-seller, and Maeve – drawing after drawing of Maeve.

By the end of the war, he had an established reputation as an illustrator, with several books under his belt. He and Maeve were living with their two sons in Glebe Place in Chelsea, close to the studio he had been renting since 1941 in Manresa Road. (There had been some sort of divine hand guiding the army planners. Mervyn had spent part of 1941 posted to the Duke of York Barracks in the King's Road in Chelsea, and found the studio which he kept for all of his working life, paying £78 annual rent, while pretending to train at that time as a bomb-disposal expert. It was the least distinguished part of his army career. At one point he set light to the barracks while smoking a pipe!)

When the Peakes returned to Chelsea for good in 1945 with the army out of the way, there was a bohemian splendour to their lives. Augustus John and Peter Ustinov were virtual neighbours, and Dylan Thomas came in and out of the house. Once the infant Sebastian was walking down the King's Road and bumped into Dylan Thomas, persuading him to take him to the pictures. His parents were later astonished by the feat, because Dylan Thomas was famous for never having any money, but on that day the impecunious Welsh poet agreed to the request by the artist's son, and they sat watching one of the

Fabian and Sebastian Peake with 'antlers'.

from the telephone directory. When the phone was answered, they would pretend to be from London Transport reporting that a family member had been killed in a bus accident. According to Sebastian, his father fell out with Graham Greene over that. Sebastian says that his father, who was fond of Jacques Tati and Groucho Marx, did not like jokes which actually frightened people. 'One of his tricks was to take one end of an extremely long professional tape measure into Regent Street. He'd meet somebody in the street and say that he was from Westminster Council and his colleague was unfortunately ill, and ask them to hold this end of the tape measure because "We have to measure this part of Lower Regent Street." Then he would walk to the very end, and give the other end of the tape to some other person. Then he would cross the road and sit in the Kardomah café and wait to see how long these two people would stay holding the two ends of the tape measure.'

very first showings of Disney's *Dumbo,* the story of the elephant who flies with his ears.

Mervyn Peake used to enjoy practical jokes. One night Graham Greene and Dylan Thomas sat in the Peakes' house phoning random numbers

Sebastian believes that Steerpike's practical jokes were an extension of what his father had done. The innocent in the Kardomah café became a much more scheming character in the book, but the parallel is there. Sebastian says, 'There is a type of literary voyeurism in Steerpike seen from my father's point of view, which is an extrapolation in a way of the many practical

Painting of Sark by Mervyn Peake.
'Illustrating, writing, walking, climbing up trees and down to remote bays, watching schools of dolphins, hearing the screech of sea-gulls, puffin landing, all of this world entered everything upon which Mervyn embarked.'
Maeve Gilmore

Mervyn Peake with one of
his white cats.
*Steerpike had imagined he
had heard a heavy, deep
throbbing, a monotonous
sea-like drumming of
sound ... the deep
unhurried purring was like
the voice of an ocean in
the throat of a shell.*
(*Titus Groan*: 'The Stone
Lanes')

jokes he used to play.'

The Peakes were popular and went to lots of
parties. Clare remembers her father as having lots
of female friends, and they were not always
glamorous. In a telling and sweet memory she
says that he could make plain people feel that
they were beautiful. He had natural English good
manners. She says, 'He was completely
unconventional and conventional at the same
time. He couldn't give a damn about whether his
shirt was ironed or his socks matched or his
dinner was on the table or anything, but he
hated rudeness or arrogance or unkindness.
Those were the things he would tell me not to
be.'

But he sought solitude too, and in 1946 he
took his family back to live on Sark, that other
world reached only through the tunnel in the
rock face, returning to draw inspiration from the

same well which had served him a decade
before. Material pleasures were never a priority,
which was fortunate, because they moved to a
giant house with no electricity, and water only
from a pump in the garden. It had been the
headquarters of the German occupation force on
Sark, and for the next four years became home
for the Peakes.

For the children, it was an extraordinary
upbringing. By law, there are no cars on the
island, so they could run everywhere unhindered.
Clare was born in le Chalet, the big house they
lived in, amid scenes of such bohemian squalor
that the nanny hired to look after her left on the
day of her birth. The exact provocation was the
appearance of Judy, the family's pet donkey, who
wandered into the bedroom to see what all the
fuss was about!

But they were blissfully happy, for most of
the time, apart from Sebastian, when he was
forced away from this paradise to a rather grim
boarding school on Guernsey. Mervyn Peake
worked away on *Gormenghast*, the second book
in the trilogy, and the house filled with paintings
and stuffed birds, and amethysts, and things he
found on the beach. Mervyn showed his sons the
places he had found in the 1930s. Sebastian
remembers being shown the way down to the
coupée bay, by the sheer south side of the
coupée, the narrow cliff which joined the two
ends of Sark, to harvest 'omers', big shellfish a
bit like oysters. Mervyn had a fully-grown palm
tree shipped in and planted it in the garden,
which the children would play on as pirates.

He worked in one room of the house, but his
children remember that they could interrupt him
without being shouted at. He constantly had
different projects on the go, continually painting
and then repainting over canvasses if he was not
happy with them, drawing and illustrating, often
dressing up his children to act as models, and
writing *Gormenghast*. He never worked on the
prose on its own; it was always surrounded by
drawings and notes.

While they were on Sark, he would stop
working once a week, and do a special drawing
for Fabian and Sebastian in a book they kept for
the purpose. But in a time of paper shortage, the
books he used to write in came from anywhere.
If he could not get hold of a 'publisher's dummy',
he would find a second-hand book and stick
paper over the pages, so that he had a book to
write in. The manuscript for an unfinished play,
based on the character of *Gormenghast*'s
Headmaster Bellgrove, is written on pages stuck

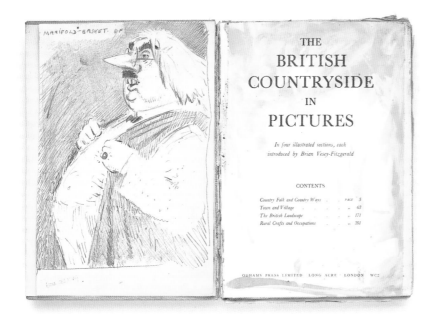

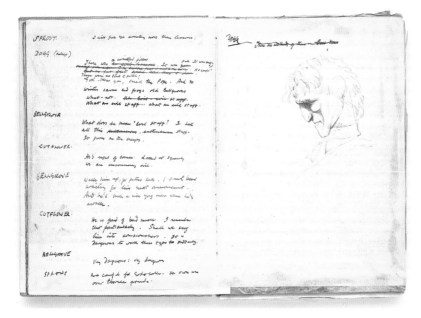

top: *The British Countryside in Pictures* recycled as an exercise book. 'Manifold basket' was a comic idea which Mervyn Peake developed after hearing there was a problem with the 'manifold gasket' on his car.

above: Sketches for an unfinished Gormenghast play with Bellgrove as the main character.

Little Sark begins and the Bluff narrows. Between the Twins would be water now.' These strange names are all places on Sark. It is as if the epic flood which threatens the very existence of the castle is the sea around Sark.

For Maeve, Sark was perfection. She wrote, 'It was not far from *Titus*, this world where the mist hid one from another, and the wind howled as violently as the scarecrow dogs in the outer dwellings of Gormenghast, and the fog-horns wailed as one could imagine 'The (Wild) Thing' in her melancholy … All of this world entered everything upon which Mervyn embarked.'

Another reason why he was attracted to Sark may lie in his upbringing in China. Sark is a strange and beautiful place, a world of its own, set apart from the mainstream. Other former colonial residents have settled in the Channel Islands, and not just for tax reasons. They have wanted to keep a foot overseas, while keeping England in view. For Mervyn Peake, Sark may have been a sort of psychological pressure chamber, clearing the bubbles from his system as it were, after being a student, and then after the war. Even after his family were living back in England, he returned to Sark again on his own in 1956, when he was trying to complete the third volume in the trilogy, *Titus Alone*.

The Peakes were happy on Sark for that period after the end of the war, but it could not last. The kitchen table, which they bought on Sark for ten shillings, and the white cats, and hundreds of paintings and drawings, were all shovelled for a while into his Chelsea studio, before they found a flat on the Embankment. The reason they came back was the most prosaic of all; they needed to earn some money. Mervyn Peake was definably not a tax exile in the Channel Islands. He hardly earned enough to pay any taxes all his life.

Back in London, he started teaching again. *Gormenghast*, the second book in the trilogy came out, and for that, and a volume of poetry, *The Glassblowers*, he won a Royal Society of Literature Award of £100. They moved for a while to a large house in Kent, but could never afford it; the RSL award did not do much to help pay the mortgage. So they all moved back again to his studio in Manresa Road in Chelsea. It was a purpose-built Victorian studio, just a giant room with a huge northern window, in a block of half a dozen set on two floors with a corridor joining each studio. A big stove brought the only warmth in winter. The rent remained small, and the memory of it is a glimpse into another age,

into a book called *The British Countryside in Pictures*. When he stuck the pages in, Mervyn Peake left a few photographs in view, so that among the pages of dialogue for his play there are pictures of sturdy farm-hands scything corn. Fabian remembers his father drawing a sketch on one side of a piece of paper, then writing on the other, and sticking it into one of his hardback books, obliterating the drawing.

There are curious specific references to locations on Sark in the Gormenghast books – the margins of the castle are as **'irregular as the coastline of a squall-rent island'**. And more specifically Gertrude interrogates Titus as to where exactly he has seen the usurper Steerpike: **'You have been in the North headstones beyond Gory and the Silver Mines. I know where you've been. You've been to the Twin Fingers where**

TITUS GROAN

by Mervyn Peake

Second Impression, 15s net

"The merit of the book lies . . . in the boldness of its attempt. It has not been written in obedience to any fashionable school. It is not timid; it does not safeguard itself against attack by the desiccated anti-romantics; it does not sneer or hedge . . . Mr. Peake throws in all his forces of dream, vision and language."
CHARLES MORGAN in the *Sunday Times*

"Mr. Mervyn Peake's fancy runs to the vast, the sombre, the saturnine, the darkly opulent, the fearsomely comic, the Gothic, the ghoulish, the pictorially macabre. He has a poet's feeling . . . for words and a tense descriptive power."
The Times Literary Supplement

"I am forced to say that Mr. Peake's first novel holds me with a glittering eye . . . I do not think I have ever so much enjoyed a novel sent to me for review . . . it persuades you to read on . . . gigantic set pieces of action . . . magnificently thrilling."
HENRY REED in the *New Statesman*

"Written in a splendid prose full of elegance and colour; though a creation of the most astonishing fancy it contains no obscurities of any kind . . . an authentic work of art."
MAURICE COLLIS in *Time and Tide*

"Mr. Peake once again creates a gallery of gnarled human grotesques; but this time he works in words instead of line . . . poetry flows through his volcanic writing; the lyrical and the monstrous are interknotted in his scenes, in the arabesques of his prose."
ELIZABETH BOWEN in *The Tatler*

". . . This crazy, decadent, yet oddly enthralling world, whose flamboyant originality haunts the imagination long after the book is laid aside."
John O' London's

"This book is a cobwebby, candle-lit escape from life."
JOHN BETJEMAN in the *Daily Herald*

"An astonishing concentration of invention and colour."
LIONEL HALE in the *Observer*

EYRE & SPOTTISWOODE · PUBLISHERS · LTD
15 BEDFORD STREET, LONDON, W.C.2

Mervyn Peake's design for the first edition of *Gormenghast*.

kinder and more rounded than our own, when artists could afford such things.

When they lived there in the early 1950s, the boys were still boarding on Guernsey, but somehow they all managed to squeeze into the big studio room in the holidays. Clare, who was still a toddler, would sleep in a little tent they built in the middle of the room, and went to the same nursery school that her brothers had been to almost a decade before at the end of the war. Although it was, according to Maeve, 'in some ways ... one of the happiest times', they could clearly not live there for long, so in 1953 they moved to Mervyn's parents' house in Wallington, in the Surrey suburbs south of London, which had been left to them when Dr Peake died the year before. It was a huge Victorian folly, with a dozen rooms, and secret tunnels and attics. Sebastian and Fabian played rock and roll in the abandoned air-raid shelter, and Clare had the stability of a childhood in one place.

Looking back now, she says she always found the house a little frightening, because of its rambling scale. But its turrets and balconies were perfect for childhood games. She remembers pretending to be a damsel in distress

with her friends, looking out from a little balcony with mock fortifications built on it, and lowering a basket which her parents filled with apples. At birthday parties, her father would do little drawings of her friends, which they took home with them; it was better than a party bag.

Mervyn continued to play practical jokes. There was a bus-stop outside the house, and he would glue a ten-shilling note to the pavement, sitting in an upstairs window to watch as people waiting in the bus queue surreptitiously tried to pick it up!

By now, Mervyn was convinced that the way to make money was to write plays. He was working on several, and finished one, *The Wit to Woo*. He sent it to Lawrence Olivier who he had first met and drawn in Germany when he was coming back from his assignment as a war artist. Olivier's reply was complimentary of Mervyn's other work, but he bluntly told him that *The Wit to Woo* was not going to be successful on the stage.

Olivier was prophetically right, and although he did help to get the play put on, it took seven years before it was accepted, and it ran for just a fortnight, making £17. Kenneth Williams starred

TITUS ALONE

MERVYN PEAKE

Eyre & Spottiswoode

in it, and the audience seemed to like it, but the reviews were indifferent, so it folded. Not only was it not the answer to their cash problems which Mervyn had hoped it would be, but it contributed to a major change in his life, the spiral down into twelve years of debilitating illness, and death.

Whether it was the disappointment of the reviews, or the anticlimax which *The Wit to Woo* became, after so many years of trying to get it staged, or just a coincidence, Mervyn Peake fell ill on the morning after it opened, and was never fully to recover again. A few days later he totally collapsed. Clare remembers the horror of that morning as if it was yesterday: 'I came down and saw him in this chair with my mother standing near him. She looked fantastically worried, and he was just absolutely shaking. There were people all around him, and then my mother looked up and saw me and called for my brothers to take me out, and when I came home he had already been taken to hospital. From that exact second on, nothing was normal again.'

Mervyn's ill-fated attempt to become a playwright had been prompted, as much as anything, by a desire to make money. It is understandable that the anticlimax of the indifferent reviews must have crushed this restless, independent spirit. He wrote from

hospital, 'Maeve! Never! Never again! It has done something to me. I have played too much around the edge of madness – oh I could cry to be free.'

The diagnosis of Peake's illness was complicated, and would probably have been different today. Some of the doctors who treated him believed that he may even have been suffering from a rare virus, *encephalitis lethargica*, dormant in his body for all of his life. There had been an outbreak of it during his childhood in China. But he suffered from Parkinson's Disease too. It meant that this vibrant, creative spirit was crushed bit by bit, ageing visibly every year. He had an operation on his brain, which in hindsight was probably not the best treatment. But he stabilised and for a few years could live mostly at home, even continuing to teach for a while, coming up and down on the train to London. By then Fabian was an art student, and would travel with his father. Mervyn was still planning and working. He had a project called 'Headhunting', which involved collecting interesting faces for an exhibition and a book, and he would draw his fellow commuters. He finished *Titus Alone*, the third volume of the Gormenghast trilogy, and it was published in 1959. It is written in a far more impressionistic and poetic style than the other two books, telling of Titus's life after he leaves the castle, and it does not feature in the BBC drama, which deals only with the first two books.

Nothing could slow the development of the illnesses which dragged him down and down. His family were fiercely protective. Clare had a schoolfriend who would come and help. She says, 'When I think about her now she was just a little girl. We would wash his face and help him get dressed and try and take him out. He would try and play football with us.' But soon he could not be looked after at home, and he went through a series of better or worse institutions, before he was finally cared for in a hospice in Burford near Oxford, run by Maeve's younger brother, Dr James Gilmore. He kept the personal charm and dignity which his friends and family had always cherished. To the end he would rise and shake the hand of a visitor, even if by then he could not outwardly recognise people he loved. The light was going out. When he died in 1968, premature senility had turned him into a very old man. The man who once lit up a room with a smile and a Groucho Marx walk, now looked older than the octogenarians who he spent his last years with.

When he died he was still only fifty-seven.

Flay

Christopher Lee

I used to meet Mervyn Peake in Harrods library in the days when there was one. It has long since gone, unfortunately. He was the most charming man, a gentle person, with a very quiet voice and the most extraordinary blue eyes. They were hooded at the sides, they went right down. It was most unusual – not the sort of thing you forget.

This is the most

Christopher Lee as Flay.
It did not look as though such a bony face as this could give normal utterance, but rather that instead of sounds, something more brittle, more ancient, something drier, would emerge, something perhaps more in the nature of a splinter or a fragment of stone. Nevertheless, the harsh lips parted. 'It's me,' he said.
(*Titus Groan*: 'The Hall of the Bright Carvings')

extraordinary story, the most important thing the BBC have ever done, quite frankly (and I am including things like the *Forsyte Saga*, *Elizabeth R*, and *Henry VIII*). In most films, the story has become so submerged in special effects over the years that there is virtually no acting

below: Mervyn Peake drawing of Flay.
He must surely have been made for the woods, so congruously had he become dissolved into a world of branches.
(*Gormenghast*: ch. 44)

required; you do your acting to a blue screen. But with *Gormenghast* it is different. We are reacting to each other. And, grotesque as it is, I find everyone in this film to be totally and completely believable.

I was chatting to a writer friend of mine, and I told him what I was doing, and he was astonished. He said, 'My god, I wouldn't have thought it was

possible.' This is almost everybody's reaction who knows Mervyn Peake's writing, which is totally unique. He has invented a style of writing and a style of prose.

Flay I think really *is* Gormenghast. He represents Gormenghast, past and present, more than anyone else in the story. Obviously his father, grandfather, great grandfather etc., etc., etc., have always been in the service of the Earl, as now he serves the seventy-seventh Earl. He is of the ages and ageless.

After he is banished to the cave, he is solitary and abandoned but he knows what is going on; he has kept an eye on Gormenghast through his telescope and he recognises Titus. And when

the boy grows up he is trying to protect him. He is a bit like Merlin locked up in his cave – the wisest person in the book. When Titus says, 'I hate Gormenghast,' this of course appals Flay. 'Oh no, no, no, can't, Lordship, can't,' and so on and so on.

The main difficulty, as far as I am concerned, is how he talks. It is not the voice so much as the

structure of Flay's speech which is unlike anybody else's you've ever heard. It is like listening to someone who is trying to learn how to talk. He is almost incoherent. This is difficult for an actor, because if you have got a simple grammatical sentence where you say to somebody, 'Look, you are one of Swelter's kitchen rats, aren't you?' and he says, 'Yes,' then it is much easier. But in this I say 'Leave Swelter in fat and grease' – it's a strange line. And then: 'Not fit for the stones – you,' or 'No time for you. Swelter, never Swelter in stone lanes.' This extraordinary staccato way of breaking up words is unlike anything I have ever done. It is hard to make it mean something, so that the meaning

transcends the lack of grammar.

The other thing that is distinctive about Flay in the book is the sound he makes when he walks. His knee joints click all the time. But obviously you can't do that on film. It would drive everybody crazy. Every time you move – 'click, click'. The audience simply wouldn't accept it, it would become very irritating. So the only thing I've been able to do is to throw my lower leg forward on every step, as if he walks in a strange way. It's hard to do when you are going backwards!

The imagination is of the *fantastick* with a 'k' on the end, as they used to call it in Shakespearean days. To have that kind of mind, to be able to invent an entire historical era without really defining it, says a great deal for his amazing powers of invention and imagination. Is it seventeenth, eighteenth or nineteenth century? There is no definition as far as the historical period is concerned. To me a French word, *grotesquerie*, sums it up.

I wouldn't make any comparisons with the gothic films which I did forty years ago. They were imaginary, but this has every conceivable kind of emotion. It is sad, it is extremely funny, it is very frightening, it is vicious, particularly of course in the character of Steerpike. There may be a kind of gothic atmosphere, but there is no other similarity, none whatsoever. You can't compare the work of Mervyn Peake with that of Bram Stoker or even Edgar Allan Poe or any of these writers. He is unique.

Christopher Lee has been a film actor for more than fifty years, in parts ranging from Scaramanga in *The Man with the Golden Gun* and Count Dracula to Prince Philip. His most recent major role was as Jinnah in a film about the founder of Pakistan.

Chapter 3

'Fantastic Realism'

When *Titus Groan* came out at the end of the Second World War, it jostled for position alongside other new works in the first years of the peace, books like T.S. Eliot's *The Four Quartets*, Evelyn Waugh's *Brideshead Revisited* and George Orwell's *Animal Farm* and *1984*. It was the pivotal moment of the twentieth century, the transition from war to peace, when nothing would be the same as it had been before. The cosy comfort of the class structure, country-house England, the Empire itself, had been challenged by the First World War, and were broken for ever in the Second World War. As the world outside was burning, Mervyn Peake built a parallel internal world with its own rituals, manners and intrigues.

The reviews for *Titus Groan* were generally very positive, although the very first reviewer, a man called Edward Shanks, did not like it, and that left a nasty taste with Mervyn and Maeve. Mervyn wanted to send him a telegram saying 'Shanks a million!' For her part, Maeve harboured a grudge for years. She had a lifelong sense that Mervyn was not regarded at his true worth.

The appeal of the book at that time, to most reviewers apart from Mr Shanks, defined itself in a kind of escapism, just what was needed after the slaughter of the war. For John Betjeman it was 'a cobwebby, candle-lit escape from life'. And when the second volume, *Gormenghast* itself, came out four years later, again to critical acclaim, and the Royal Society of Literature Award, Mervyn's place seemed assured. Orson Welles wrote of *Gormenghast*, 'I read the book with immense pleasure … It is in every way a remarkable work, and I look forward to re-reading it, as well as *Titus Groan*.' Anthony Burgess, who had the novel in his '99 best books since 1939', wrote a thoughtful essay, which appeared as an introduction to a later edition of *Titus Groan*. Burgess called it 'a rich wine of fancy chilled by the intellect to just the right temperature. There is no really close relative to it in all our prose

literature. It is uniquely brilliant, and we are right to call it a modern classic.'

This was a time when the templates of the political landscape were shifting, as Eastern Europe was absorbed into the communist sphere. But although Steerpike is a rebel and the book examined social and class inequality, there was little comfort for Marxists. The critic for the left-wing *New Statesman*, Henry Reed, was reluctant to see a political parallel in the relationship between the Groans and the Bright Carvers: 'Even a Marxist might find so riotous an embellishment of his favourite theme a little frivolous.'

The vision is so singular that there were enormous problems, then as now, putting the books into a satisfactory category. Mervyn Peake's sheer versatility could work against him. The *Spectator* critic of the Gormenghast books called him 'a genius with two nibs', a compliment with a double edge. If he did not decide which 'nib' was the more important, then would his legacy last? Mervyn's brother, Leslie, saw him as an artist first, and a poet second – the novels came third. He told the biographer John Watney, 'I know that it is upon the novels that his reputation rests; but I think that in time it will be upon his drawings and his poetry that his real fame will be founded.'

The difficulty Mervyn Peake had in getting accepted by the mainstream was understandable. He *knew* he was doing something different. Indeed, he *wanted* to do something different. He wrote to his friend Gordon Smith about the problems he had in realising his giant epic, offering a rare and tantalising glimpse into what he thought was behind it:

'What *was* I after anyway? I suppose, to create a world of my own in which those who belong to it and move in it come to life and never step outside into either *this* world of bus queues, ration-books, or even the Upper Ganges – or into *another* imaginative world.'

He wanted the book to have a *tone* of its

opposite: 'My husband is now an owl, Master Chalk. I'd say it was an improvement.'
Gertrude

'Babies?' said Mrs Slagg ... 'I could eat the little darlings, sir, I could eat them up!' (*Titus Groan*: 'Prunesquallor's Knee-cap')

own. So that the moods, although varied, would have a consistency. He and Gordon Smith had always used a sort of shorthand, quoting from the characteristics of imaginary animals, and in this letter he said that *Titus Groan* should be identifiable like one of the animals, a gryphon, for example: **' ... a gryphon that may have a complex temperament and show different coloured scales under different lights – but whose smell must pervade every page – sometimes like Gryphonodour, sometimes Gryphonstench – sometimes Gryphon-of-roses. This I don't think I've done. Maybe I'll have to hack it to hell and re-write whole chapters. It gets too sane in the middle of the book, and the saner it gets – in other words the more it gets like a novel in the library subscribers' sense of the word, the more superficial it becomes. At its strangest it is nearest to being spiritual – as against materialistic.**

'Damn novels in the sense of being NOVELS. I want to create between two covers a world, the movements of which – in action, atmosphere and speech – enthrall and excite the imagination.

'I know this is flying very high but I suddenly feel sick with so much of it. ... it is very like other novels. Nanny Slagg and Fuchsia

seem intolerably sentimental. Steerpike, wordy, to the verge of tears. Oh God!'

Not only was the subject matter unique, but Mervyn Peake was aiming at a prose style and structure all of his own. Anthony Burgess wrote: 'Unlike the vaunted post-war names, he does not seek – in his subject-matter – to probe topical themes like race, class and homosexuality or advance the frontiers of what we may call the contemporary consciousness; in technique, he appears to look back rather than forward. His books nourish the private imagination.'

But in the 1950s, some critics were painfully dismissive. Kingsley Amis called Mervyn Peake a 'bad fantasy writer of maverick status'. Peake's versatility had already given him commercial problems. It had been hard to get his next novel *Mr Pye* printed, because the whimsical story about Sark was not what was expected from the creator of Gormenghast. His output had included hundreds of drawings, and illustrated books, as well as a story about pirates. Questions were asked about where he was going next.

Whether it was because of the negative influence of critics like Amis, or just the changing times, by the mid-1960s sales of the books were flagging. In 1964, with Mervyn now permanently out of the public eye because of his illness, Maeve received the inevitable letter from the publisher. 'It would apparently be impossible to publish the trilogy under 50/-. I am afraid this would be altogether too high for the fiction market ... this means allowing Gormenghast to go out of print.' But then the wind suddenly caught its sails. Penguin brought out a paperback, with Mervyn's drawings of the main characters on the front cover, and Gormenghast was discovered by a new generation. Among the new readers was Ian Richardson, who plays Lord Groan in our production. He says, 'When they came out they made a great stir, because they were so extraordinarily unusual. Already it was known that he was a dying man and this added a rather sinister, perfectly understandable frisson to reading them, and an insight into the man's mind, which must have been quite extraordinary.'

The books had emerged from a different Europe, a war which began with the last charge of the Polish Cavalry, and ended with the atomic bomb – bringing profound changes. But what the readers discovered in the Gormenghast trilogy when it re-emerged in the late 1960s was something else. A story written before youth culture was even thought of, became, and has continued to be, a sort of manifesto for restless

real – we may have some clue about the evil kitchen boy Steerpike.

The intense passion of Steerpike's desire to eliminate the unfairness of his birth, and the abuse he has suffered, turns into a destructive wind which almost brings down the castle. The story ends with a stage as full of corpses as a late Shakespearean tragedy. Our Steerpike did only one piece of reading to prepare for the part – Machiavelli's *The Prince*.

We can see the history of the century written in this character, drawing parallels with the rise of tyrants from Hitler, to Milosevic, or Saddam Hussein. As civilisation itself had been overturned by Hitler, the House of Groan is shaken and fundamentally changed by the fascist usurper Steerpike.

Mervyn Peake portrays the complexity of evil. Steerpike is an attractive, compelling character who plausibly ingratiates himself with the aristocracy of the castle. If he is pushed to categorise it, the director, Andy Wilson, defines Gormenghast as 'a speculation about the nature of evil. It is not a tract. Steerpike is not representative of a philosophical or political view. He is simply representing a character who is possessed of true evil. Hitler was said to be very charming, he had a fabulous presence and an extraordinary way with children, dogs and women. I think that's what Peake is describing in Steerpike.'

The violence in Gormenghast is real; the

youth. In the fractured culture of the last decades of the century – where American high school boys dressed themselves as cult figures from a computer game to gun down their classmates for

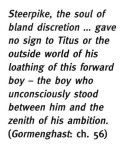

Steerpike, the soul of bland discretion ... gave no sign to Titus or the outside world of his loathing of this forward boy – the boy who unconsciously stood between him and the zenith of his ambition. (Gormenghast: ch. 56)

Storyboard to plan camera angles of the fight between Swelter and Flay, and the death of Lord Groan.

Flay and the chef were staring at one another over their master's shoulder. The three of them seemed to be moving as one piece. (*Titus Groan*: 'Blood at Midnight')

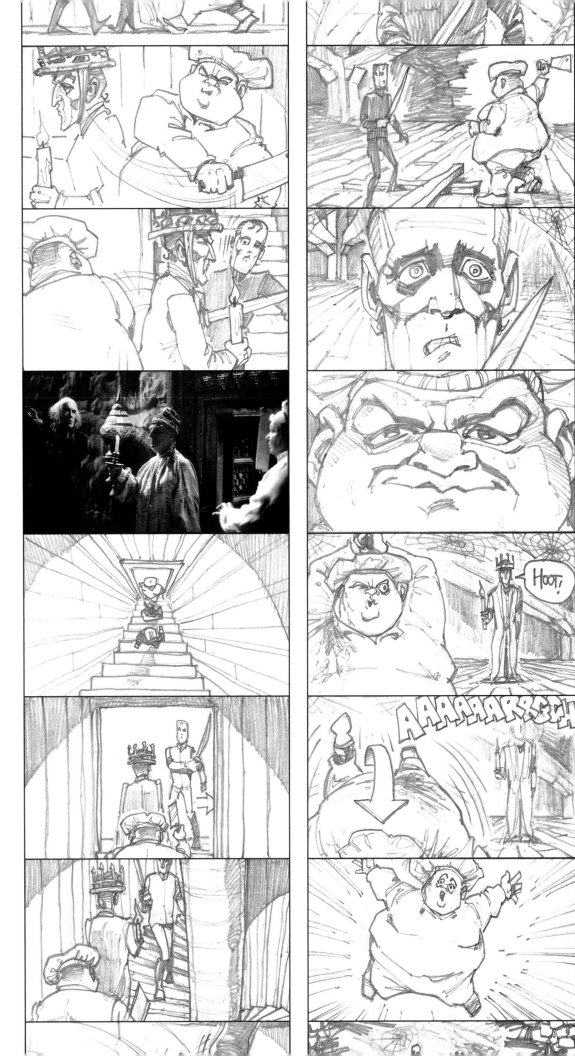

knives are sharp; there is horror. Anthony Burgess saw this very much as a reflection of the time when it was written: 'after a long and horrifying war ... the cat's claws ripping a "crimson wedge" from Steerpike's cheek ... the fight between Flay and Swelter – these are not gratuitous Gothicisms so much as reflections out of an era of horrors.'

But Mervyn Peake does not dwell on the horror; the intensity of his gaze is on the humans at either end of the knife, as villain or victim. And his biggest response to the destruction is in the humour. After the precise and surgical savagery of the fight to the death between Flay and Swelter, the fat cook falls to his death from a window, and his body exudes a giant fart as he collapses into a puddle. Gormenghast is drenched, not in blood, but in humour.

The designer of the TV adaptation, Christopher Hobbs, says that it is the human scale of the story which is important. It reminds him of Jacobean drama 'because everyone ends up dead at the end of it, or mad. But it is actually a comedy. What is bizarre about it is the

black comedy. It is just full of slapstick. Although at the same time, it is not what you'd call jolly stuff in some ways, because people are constantly being thrown out of windows and flattened!'

The librettist of a new Gormenghast opera, Duncan Fallowell, calls the books 'fantastic realism'. The people who live in Gormenghast are real, and are governed by human emotions and motivation, but it all happens in a fantastic environment that clearly does not exist anywhere in the world. It is like a bridge between the nineteenth-century novel and science fiction. Peake's 'fantastic realism' prefigures the magical realism of Latin America and India by decades.

Being ahead of its time, Gormenghast did not help the bank balance. Mervyn never made much money either as a writer or as an illustrator, although he was talked of once as the 'greatest living illustrator'. He did not live to see the renaissance of interest in the books. His last years were lived in a twilight world, his creativity dammed by disease. Maeve was trying

Richard Griffiths as Swelter 'falling out of the window', in fact filmed in front of a blue screen in the studio.

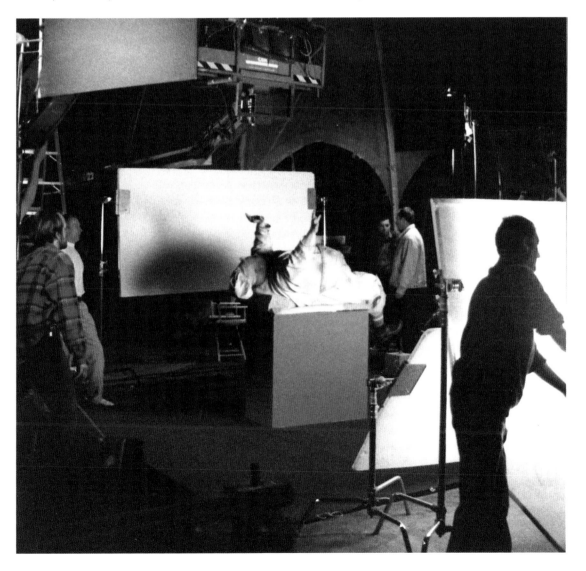

when he bought a car in the early 1950s, he was surprised to be stopped by the police several months later to be told that he needed tax and insurance!

Some of Mervyn Peake's financial problems were caused by bad luck, and the times he lived in. Nearly all of the print run of his first book, a pirate romp called *Captain Slaughterboard Drops Anchor*, was destroyed when an air raid hit the publisher's warehouse. And he was poorer for taking Graham Greene's advice in the middle of the war when he won a competition to design the logo for a new paperback company. There were to be four logos on every book published, and he was offered a farthing a logo – adding up to one penny for every book sold – or a £10 flat fee. £10 felt like a lot to a man with two small children during the war. Sebastian says that the conversation between his father and Greene must have gone something like this: 'Graham Greene said, "Take the £10 because we are in the middle of a war, and we don't know that paper is ever going to be available again. Supposing the Germans invade? Supposing we lose the war? How do we know books will continue?"' So he took the £10, and the paperback publisher, which was Pan Books, turned into a major success, with four of Mervyn Peake's little pictures of Pan

above and right: Mervyn Peake drawings for unfinished Gormenghast opera.

everything, to keep his name in the public eye, and to keep his books in print, while engaged in the spiritually and materially draining process of getting him the most appropriate medical treatment. She was never bitter, although caring for him cut out the time she could have spent on her own artistic career. For one third of the time that they were together, he was a sick man, but she carried on trying to win his work the recognition it deserved.

Soon after his death, plagued by money worries, Maeve offered everything she had of his art to the Tate Gallery, and was offered just £1,500 for the whole oeuvre. (It is a price which a single small drawing of his might fetch nowadays.) The rebuilding of Mervyn Peake's name for new generations is all down to her determination.

Sebastian Peake believes that there was not a single year of his father's working life that he made £1,000. He would have done better as a manual labourer. He had a detached attitude to some requirements of the world. For example,

opposite: Mervyn Peake's manuscript.
To win her favour he must talk her own language ... 'Today I saw a great pavement among the clouds made of grey stones, bigger than a meadow. No one goes there.'
(*Titus Groan*: 'Soap for Greasepaint')

'I hate you for coming here! I hate you in my room!' She ringed the table edge with both her hands behind her — and rattled it on its legs.

Steerpike watched her carefully)

Unimaginative himself, he could recognise imagination in her; he had come upon one whose whole nature was the contradictory of his own. He knew that behind her simplicity was something that he could never have — something he despised as impractical. Something that would never carry her to power or riches — but would retard her — and keep her apart in the world of her own make-believe. To win her favour he must talk her own language. He struck an attitude, raising one hand, and in an even, flat voice that contrasted with Fuchsia, in her agony, with her own passionate outcry, said:

"Today I saw a great pavement among the clouds — made of grey stones, bigger than a meadow. No-one goes there. Only a heron..."

Fiona Shaw as Irma
Prunesquallor.

What was it, she had inquired, over and over again, which prevented her from meeting someone who could appreciate and admire her? ... She had her long, unblemished neck. Her bosom was flat, it was true, and so were her feet, but after all a woman can't have everything. 'I move well, don't I, Alfred?' (*Gormenghast*: ch. 6)

Mervyn Peake drawing from manuscript. Barquentine raised his hot-looking, irritable eyes and dropped the cross-hatched corners of his mouth ... Steerpike found himself staring down into an upturned patch of wrinkles. In this corrugated terrain two eyes burned. In contrast to the dry sand-coloured skin they appeared grotesquely liquid, and to watch them was ordeal by water; all innocence was drowned. (*Titus Groan*: 'Barquentine and Steerpike')

playing his pipes on every book sold. As Sebastian ruefully reminisces, 'If he had taken the farthing, he certainly would have become a millionaire, like the man who invented cats-eyes!'

Mervyn wrote a radio adaptation of *Titus Groan* in the 1950s, condensing 200,000 words into a one-hour programme, and he discussed the writing of a Gormenghast opera with Benjamin Britten. He left some tantalising sketches for the libretto, although the opera was never finished. But he knew nothing of any plans to bring Gormenghast to the screen – the first approaches were made after he died.

Maeve had always wanted the BBC to film the books. But there were several other attempts first. They all struggled with the same problems – where is Gormenghast and how can a story of epic proportions be crammed into a feature film?

We started work on a version for television in 1994. The first suggestion came from Gub Neal, now head of drama at Channel Four. The timing seemed good in every sense. The length of the story lent itself much more readily to the advantages offered by a television serial. We thought we understood why other producers had failed to squeeze it into a single film.

Malcolm McKay wrote his four-hour adaptation, liberating a spine of humour from the story and remaining, in our view, remarkably

faithful to Mervyn Peake. There were some variations to create the drama – Rottcodd, the Keeper of the Bright Carvings, does not appear, but his name has been given to the Captain of the Guard. Sourdust and Barquentine, the crabby Keepers of the Ritual, become one character, although their story is much the same as in the books. We have lost the detail of the life of Keda and her lovers among the Bright Carvers. But her daughter, the Wild Thing, is still there, a wisp flying through the trees, representing liberty, sexual awakening, and life itself to the young Titus.

Television offers a particular intimacy to a group of such detailed and full-blooded characters, as rich and comedic as the best of Dickens's creations. They have a physical roundness and vitality provided by the 'genius with two nibs'. Peake once described how he distilled their spirits: **'As I went along with *Titus Groan* I made drawings from time to time which helped me visualise the characters and to imagine what sort of things they would say. The drawings were never exactly as I imagined the people, but were near enough for me to know when their voices had lost touch with their heads.'**

Christopher Lee as Flay.
Cameron Powrie as Titus.
*'I want to be free, Mr Flay.
I don't want any duties.'*
*'A wicked thing to say, my
lord, a wicked thing. ...
You are a Groan of the
blood – and the last of the
line. You must not fail the
Stones.'*
(*Gormenghast*: ch. 20)

The manuscripts are peppered with all kinds of other Peakian fancies which kept him on course, including the odd shopping list!

Like Dickens, Peake's characters, with their absurd names, are heightened and exaggerated towards the grotesque, but encompass a breadth of human experience. In *Gormenghast*, he creates the frustration and loneliness of a woman, Irma Prunesquallor, who hears the ticking of the biological clock; the powerful fascination of adolescence in the romantic and poetic, as Fuchsia falls in love with Steerpike; the urge to rebel among those who are expected to conform, as Titus fights the oppression of the ancient rituals; the desire of an older generation to cling to those rituals, as if conservatism would keep out the barbarian at the gate; the love of those who are loyal; the amazing capacity to hate of those who feud; and the destructive power of those who see themselves excluded by society.

Perhaps Maeve's instincts were right. Inside the BBC, there was the unique possibility to give the film the lengthy development time it required. We were also free to cast exactly to the essence of the characters, choosing actors who understood them, rather than following the commercial requirements of Hollywood fashion. The cost of the computer effects needed to provide the scale went down dramatically as the

technology developed, to less than a quarter of the original estimate, bringing us nearer to our vision.

Maeve died in 1983 without seeing her wish for the BBC to take on Gormenghast fulfilled. During the filming, I often imagined them both at Shepperton, sitting side by side on set in 1950s' deckchairs, relishing the action. Quite a picture. I first met the rest of the Peakes in 1997. The scripts were done and I wanted to invite them to come to the BBC for the first time. I arranged a drinks party in the office of Michael Wearing, legendary producer and commissioner of drama, who has guided *Gormenghast* as executive producer from the outset. The BBC is not a glamorous place. We stood amongst the grey metal filing cabinets, looking out over the wasteland of Shepherds Bush and the serried rows of milk floats in the Unigate car park below, whilst I agonised about the wine, Sebastian Peake being a wine merchant of some distinction. They were full of generosity and charm. But they had travelled this road before, and I wanted to tell them that this time we would do it. That somehow the wind was behind us. We would work out this lurching vision and chart a course through the rooms of their father's imagination. We would find Gormenghast and bring it to the screen.

Steerpike
Jonathan Rhys Meyers

Jonathan Rhys Meyers as Steerpike, dressed as a kitchen boy before he rises through the castle.

He must know all things, for only so might he have, when situations arose in the future, a full pack of cards to play from ... He foresaw himself in control of men. (*Titus Groan*: 'Keda and Rantel')

What can I do that has never been done to Gormenghast in all its years? Seventy-seven earls and it has never had this happen? I think it could have done with it a couple of hundred years beforehand.

I'm not trying to complicate it. I have been reading a little bit of Samuel Beckett, just for myself because I like him. He hates to colour things.

You just have to say it. If it is there, it is there. You know, that was my fear – how I am going to do this? How am I actually going to please everyone in this? And then I decided to please no one. Just do it. It has been difficult. Because I have this huge doubt and insecurity. There hasn't been one take that I have done on this, that I've not actually felt could have been better.

Steerpike is myself, he can't be anyone else. If I tried to make him somebody else, and tried to change myself totally, it would be a disaster. I don't think I would actually do it at all. The evil in him comes from loneliness, and rejection. That's something I feel. I feel this rage. Steerpike is just rejected. When you are rejected you can't accept love, and you most certainly can't give it. And if you can't give love then there is nothing really else worth it, you know? All this climbing the ladder of Gormenghast, essentially all he wants is love and respect, and this is what it brings. He thinks, 'If I am the king of this castle, everyone will love me.' So it is about wanting to be cuddled more than anything else. My childhood was one of rejection and this is what it was about. It has had its strongest effect on me. But I've gone into a career which has a lot of rejection in it, and plus I have got into my head that I want to be a great actor, which is the last thing I should have done. I don't want to be perfect, I just want to be great. Like Steerpike I would rather die than fail, and that's honest. I would rather die than fail.

It is not a very healthy way of living. And there is the sexual frustration. I'm feeling huge sexual frustration. This is another huge part of Steerpike, because he has never actually had sex. All this sexual frustration, all this doubt, all this insecurity, all this fear, all this anger and rejection is hopefully what you are getting. I hope it makes people feel something. I would rather be called extremely bad or extremely good, but never just 'all right'. If somebody is really truly, truly awful, then it is fascinating to look at. If someone is extremely, extremely good, there is also a joy in that. But when people are kind of like good-ish, alright-ish, perfectly adequate, then I think that's the worst. Mediocre. To be mediocre at anything is like pouring a bottle of water into the sea. You are just the same as every other wave.

I tell you what. I really don't know what Steerpike is, I only know myself now. I've kind of lost that part of it. Maybe for the first two weeks, I was like Johnny, Steerpike, Johnny, Steerpike, Johnny, Steerpike. And now it is really inseparable. I just can't take it off.

There are not really many things in life I want. I don't desire a car, or friends or clothes or clubbing or parties. There is a space that you can get into sometimes – and you get one or two moments during a job that you do or a script that you do, where the world just disappears and it is nothingness and it is emptiness – and it is fantastic. And it is almost like you are elevated off the ground a couple of inches, and you can't feel anything underneath you, you can't feel the clothes you are wearing, you can't even feel yourself. Emptiness is probably the highest level that you can reach, because if you are empty you are like water and it can go right through you and right back out of you and it filters, but when you have all these things inside knocking then ... that's Steerpike. Steerpike can't take something in and just let it flow out again. He takes it in and it rocks all his cages and little pieces stay in this cage, and that cage, and this cage, and that cage, and slowly it is like water going into wood; slowly it begins to rot and rot and rot and rot and rot. Because he is just not letting it flow through at all. It is the same for me.

Jonathan Rhys Meyers had no formal training as an actor. He came to international prominence when he was cast by Neil Jordan in *Michael Collins*. He has starred in eleven films, including *Velvet Goldmine*.

Chapter 4

'If You Are Going to Steal, Then Steal From the Best!'

The approach to Ladakh airport, in the northernmost region of India, is one of the most awesome in the world. On the day I flew in, the plane nearly made it once, but after circling round, and failing to find a hole in the clouds, it had to return to Jammu to land and take on fresh fuel, before going up again for another try. The airstrip, one of the highest in the world, is at 11,000 feet in a small bowl in the mountains, and surrounded by sharp peaks which are 2,000 feet higher. It feels as if the wingtips are scraping the mountainside itself as the plane does a sharp circle in order to lose enough height to land.

Ladakh's remoteness has preserved it from the modern world. In this wild and beautiful rocky landscape, a high-altitude desert plain, the air is thin, and the light a dazzling haze. They call it 'Little Tibet', stuck by an accident of history onto the top of India, and now divided for ever from Tibet itself by Chinese communist guards, who make the border more impassable than any mountain range.

Here in a remote monastery, a stone citadel clinging to the edge of a rocky outcrop, surrounded by a lunar landscape of giant boulders, I saw Gormenghast as it had been in my mind since I first read the books.

In the kitchen, a room of impossible height, where one wall was the sheer face of the mountain itself, small dark men ran to get more fuel from a giant pile of cut-down thorn bushes to stoke a raging fire. Boys, who were novice monks, laughed and played in the temple underneath fearful dark-painted images of gods with giant eyes. And in the fields around, the few areas close to the river where anything grows at all, the people of Ladakh measure the seasons of their lives in rhythm with the monasteries.

I sat in the tiny cell of a monk, on a carved wooden bed full of cupboards built into the wall, like a bunk in an old sailing ship, as he talked of a closed world in a time warp, and the ways of

The Petrified City by Max Ernst. Director's image for Gormenghast.

Ladakh – III by Serbjeet Singh. Producer's image for Gormenghast.

opposite: Design by Christopher Hobbs for the burning of the Library.

Top view of the Library building.
As for burning scene...

ater tank model.

rd roofs.

Design by Christopher Hobbs of Gormenghast Castle.

Withdrawn and ruinous it broods in umbra: the immemorial masonry: the towers, the tracts. It is all corroding? No. Through an avenue of spires a zephyr floats ... Deep in a fist of stone a doll's hand wriggles, warm rebellious on the frozen palm. A shadow shifts its length. A spider stirs ...
(*Gormenghast*: ch. 1)

prayer and ritual which bind the community together. The furniture, the kitchen utensils, everything around us, seemed to be hundreds of years old. I remembered the line from Bunyan in the front of *Titus Groan*: 'would'st thou see a man in the clouds, and have him speak to thee?'

Of course, Gormenghast is not a Buddhist monastery, but neither is it an English castle. And surely, here in the other worldliness of Ladakh, we can glimpse something of China before the

communists, the China of Mervyn Peake's childhood, which Maeve said 'influenced a mind which from somewhere had a vision that finally betrayed it by its richness'. I returned to London to find that Andy Wilson, the director, had found his own Gormenghast in a picture by Max Ernst called *The Petrified City*. It had curious similarities to the picture I had brought back from Ladakh: the one a modern image by a prophetic twentieth-century artist; the other the timeless harmony of an enclosed society.

Design by Christopher Hobbs of Nannie Slagg going out of the castle to see the Bright Carvers.
'A new little Groan has been born, a little boy. A little boy of the Blood. I am in charge, of course, and I want a wet nurse for him at once.'
(*Titus Groan*: 'Mrs Slagg by Moonlight')

Design by Christopher
Hobbs for the Balcony
overlooking the Courtyard.

'People are very frightened
nowadays because things
change so fast that they
find it very difficult to
keep up, so they are
comforted when they go to
these great stable places
like Mount Athos. There
aren't many of them left,
and some are little more
than dreams anyway, but I
wanted to get the feeling
in *Gormenghast* of a place
which has gone on and
on, and is threatened. I
am sure that is part of
what the book is about –
the threat to stability. In
the third book, Titus
almost goes back, just to
make sure that
Gormenghast is still there.
He turns away from it; but
it's very important that it
is there. Gormenghast is
that imaginary place which
never changes. The rituals
don't seem to be religious
rituals. So it actually
steers clear of any
iconography of that sort,
leaving it completely open.'
Christopher Hobbs,
designer.

These were the first two things we showed
Christopher Hobbs when he joined us as designer
of *Gormenghast*. They prompted him to look out
a picture of Mount Athos, the Greek monastery
on an isolated peninsula, which is a fusion of
influences from East and West. And then the
images of what we were looking for began to
pile up, pictures which showed a universality in
architecture, common solutions across the world
to the same problems of how to use natural
materials for shelter and protection, and beauty.
There were pictures from Isfahan in Ancient
Persia, villages in Morocco, Santa Sophia, the
giant Byzantine Cathedral, gardens in Italy,

churches in Spain, and landscapes from China –
inspiring a Gormenghast which is everywhere and
nowhere, otherworldly but accessible:
recognisable in the universality of its borrowed
references. Christopher became a cultural magpie,
seeking jewels from across the world, a colour
here, a fabric there, a cornice from England,
texture from Tibet. He wanted to build a set
which looked strange but familiar, unique but
universal.

Mervyn Peake was adamant that
Gormenghast was not a particular place.
Disarmingly he once said, **'If I had set the story
in Paddington, I should have been restricted by
the need for urban accuracy.'** Since nearly all of
the sets for the film were built in the studio,
there were no external concerns, and no limits to
the imagination, except the budget.

In the spirit of Peake, Christopher painted his
way into *Gormenghast*, producing detailed and
highly coloured set drawings at an early stage.
But first he had made a collage of pictures of
monasteries and mountains, fortresses and
castles, which he had cut out from magazines
and stuck onto card. This rather simple image
stayed on the wall above his desk throughout
the production. The details came from Yemen,

Christopher Hobbs's collage of the influences which inspired Gormenghast Castle.

Jonathan Rhys Meyers as Steerpike. Zoë Wanamaker as Clarice, Lynsey Baxter as Cora. The 'ageless' walls of the room are made of insulation foam.

Greece and Tibet, but look as if they could have been built in the same place. They belong to a 'world castle architecture'. High walls with wooden balconies and towers on top have been common across the world, from Norman England, to Mount Athos and Ladakh. They are good for defence, against the weather as well as armed enemies. Our aim was to translate this into a solid castle with elements which echo known places, without being defined as coming from a single castle.

In his book *Drawings*, published just before *Gormenghast*, Peake compares the authority of a good drawing to that of a **'prince, who with a line of Kings for lineage can make no gesture that does not recall some royal ancestor'**. This was the kind of integrity within a world which Christopher set out to create.

Turning this elusive vision into reality required ingenuity, a lot of luck – and a warehouse full of Rajasthani doorways! The doorways, giant blocks of wood which are intricately carved, came from a friend of Christopher, who has an antiques stall on Camden Lock. It turned out that he had dozens of pieces of wooden Indian furniture stored in a

dusty building in Gloucestershire. As well as the door frames themselves, we acquired shutters, door posts and wooden cupboards, which gave the whole set a borrowed permanence. Some of the door frames on the set were made from cupboards. Because they were small, they helped to make the walls look bigger, informing the scale of the whole castle. The aim was that if we put them in the right place then they would look authentic. Christopher's hope was that after looking at the film, someone would ask 'What *location* did you use?'

Buying a job lot of ancient doors turned out

Mervyn Peake manuscript.
The wind was gone and the mists were gone and the clouds were gone and the day was warm and young, and Titus was on the slopes of Gormenghast Mountain.
(*Gormenghast:* ch. 15)

to be much cheaper than carving them out of polystyrene (the usual Hollywood solution) and they looked much better. The texture of ancient wood cannot easily be replicated. But the high walls above the doorways were not real, for the simple reason that they would have been too heavy. They were designed to look like plaster on stonework which has been limewashed for hundreds of years. In fact they were done in a day by industrial sprayers using insulation foam! The foam is manufactured for builders, and designed to be squeezed into wall cavities, but the companies who do it have discovered a useful side-line in the film industry. It gives an ageless effect in an instant, and it is very light, which means that huge walls can be moved around easily.

One of the biggest sets, for the Great Hall of the castle, is a simple space, with the 'foam insulation' castle walls lining the sides of one of the largest stages at Shepperton. Hanging along the walls are long drapes with patterns inspired by Kandinsky. There are details here, and on a number of other sets, which pay homage to Paul Klee, Picasso and other key twentieth-century artists. They are not actual copies of anything but they are in the style of various artists – a great Christopher Hobbs principle: 'If you are going to steal, then steal from the best!' Since the artists of the twentieth century were often influenced by ancient and tribal art, the images looked perfectly at home in Gormenghast. You dust them down and put a cobweb here and there, and they

become acceptable in the ageless surroundings of the castle.

The film opens in a more intimate space, the first also to be built: Gertrude's bedroom, as Titus is born. There are open windows high up for birds to fly through, and ivy growing *inside* on textured red walls. Since it is Lady Groan's room it has to be very grand, with a giant bed. Mervyn Peake describes the ruin which would come in a room which has never been looked

Design by Christopher Hobbs for the twins' room, inspired by Paul Klee.

GERTRUDE'S BEDROOM

Gertrudes Room.
Bullet shaped room with
ribs & triangular windows.
Rotting red walls with
perches between the ribs.
heavy mouldering
furniture.
Interior ivy.
Birdshit and
candle drippings
everywhere.

above: Design by Christopher Hobbs for Gertrude's bedroom. The same structure was used for three sets.

Like a spider suspended by a metal cord, a candelabrum presided over the room ... long stalactites of wax lowered their pale spliths drip, drip by drip. A rough table, with a drawer half open which appeared to be full of birdseed, was in such a position below the iron spider that a cone of tallow was mounting by degrees at one corner into a lambent pyramid the size of a hat. The room was untidy to the extent of being a shambles.
(Titus Groan: 'Tallow and Birdseed')

right: Celia Imrie as Gertrude. June Brown as Nannie Slagg.
'Bring him back when he is six.'

after, covered in candle wax and great piles of birdseed and droppings, and Christopher added the shape, an octagon which has a stone coronet on the top in the exterior shot of the roofs, to mark it as the bedroom of the Countess.

It is tempting to see Gertrude, and the other Groans, as an allegory of the Royal Family. But when we planned this bedroom, Christopher saw a much more elemental figure than Queen Elizabeth II living in here: ' ... a mother earth figure in a sense. She is life, but on a very primitive level. She is rather like nature in that it is red in tooth and claw and very unforgiving,

cruel and implacable, but nevertheless we can't do anything about it. She is a sort of fertility goddess.'

Gertrude's other room, the cat room, is the same octagonal shape. The set was created inside the same structure. This time the walls are blue, painted in swirling curlicues, partly inspired by a Moroccan design, but also borrowing from Greece, and using mud architecture which seems to come from somewhere more primitive. Little rounded shapes and niches look as if the cats have rounded them off themselves. And then Christopher added a master stroke – a chandelier with goldfish swimming around in the glass shades. The idea is not in the books, but it is a visual joke in the style of Peake. The inspiration comes from a party in Isfahan in Persia in the nineteenth century, where a Sultan had goldfish in lamps, to show off his great wealth, and they seemed to be highly appropriate in a cat room.

revelation of the bright colours of the original ceiling shocked the public. In *Gormenghast*, we have tried to strike a balance between new, bright colours, and colours which would have faded. We have used handmade dyes and a lot of Indian materials which helped, because even when they are bright, they do not come over as garish.

Once, when he was in North Wales, researching material for an exhibition, Christopher was shown an old tent rolled up in the corner of a chapel. It turned out to be a relic from the Raj, a tent seized from the legendary Indian warrior king, Tipu Sahib. The floral design was still bright 200 years later, and the owners showed him a picture taken when it had been put up. Christopher looked at the bright colours, and realised that beautiful though it was, they had actually put the tent up *inside out*. The white should have been *outside* to reflect the bright Mysore sun, which would have shone through to light up the flowers painted on the inside.

The idea stayed with him, and the luminous quality of that lighting is used for the design of the pavilion where Titus is baptised – the third sight of the octagonal frame, which had already been used for the cat room and Gertrude's bedroom. These 'transformer' sets, which turn into each other, are integral to the Gormenghast design. With around 120 sets in all, it was the only way we could afford to make such an ambitious film on a BBC budget. For the baptism,

Christopher Hobbs planning the miniature world which would end up looking like the massive bulk of Gormenghast.

It was a key part of the look of Gormenghast that it was not set in a dark and dingy Victorian England. We wanted to use a palette of colours mixed in the twentieth century, and Christopher was keen not to pander to any expectations that 'old' meant 'dark'. He recalled the upset which the restored Sistine Chapel caused, when the

Design by Christopher Hobbs for the cat room – the second use of the same basic set.

Redress of Gertrude's room,
Pale 'Moroccan Blue' walls with purple-black
decorations. Moghul style fish & bird paintings
'Chinese' lantern with fish in suspended bowls to throw fish shadows

Big Fat Cushions

Design by Christopher Hobbs for Lord Groan's bedroom.

Design by Christopher Hobbs for Fuchsia's attic. *As the pearl diver murmurs, 'I am home' as he moves dimly in strange water-lights, and as the painter mutters, 'I am me' on his lone raft of floorboards, so the slow landsman on his acre'd marl – says with dark Fuchsia on her twisting staircase, 'I am home.'* (*Titus Groan*: 'The Attic')

The model for the baptism pavilion.

cultural landscape. He sees the Groan family as the British Raj, or maybe even the Mogul emperors who ruled India before them – a conquering race whose dynamism is running out. That understanding gave a consistency to the ideas, so that, for instance, Lord Groan's bedroom was developed from rooms Christopher remembers seeing in country houses in his childhood: an Edwardian lord's room with stuffed animals everywhere; a great golden bed, which is half way between an Indian temple and an Elizabethan four-poster; tiger skins on the floor.

Despite our desire not to make the past a wash of beige and sepia, there are dusty and faded colours in Fuchsia's attic, contrasting with the splash of strong colour in her scarlet dress. Looking at this set it became clear that Fuchsia in a way represents the artist, surrounded by *objets trouvés*, the sort of thing you might find in a painter's studio. She lives in an imaginative world, Peake's world. She writes all over the walls, and Christopher added a little 'Fuchsiaesque' poetry of his own, in the absence of enough original Peake!

As the world grew from imagination and drawings into sets at Shepperton, Christopher's office filled up with all kinds of objects which found their way into the film. Sitting on his desk was his bath sponge, which reminded him of a Max Ernst painting of a stone forest. On the floor was the small Moroccan goatskin lampshade

there was room for a band, a choir, and the Groan family and retainers, surrounding a beautiful Indian bronze bowl in the centre.

Christopher spent some time abroad as a child, and identified with much of Mervyn Peake's

BARQUENTINES OFFICE

1·12·98.   (21)

Painting with eyeholes cut for Steerpike's mirrors

CORMENGHAST CASTLE XIII

Barquentine's office

Stone floor. Huge Pale maps of Gormenghast around the walls, and tall filing shelves stuffed untidily with papers. Mountains of manuscript & an Autumn of loose leaves.

Reverse: Door between filing shelves.

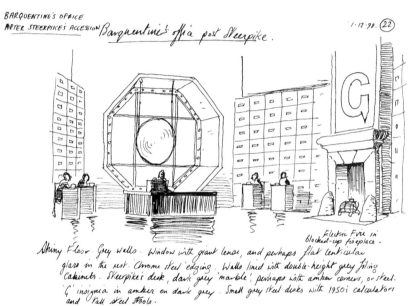

BARQUENTINE'S OFFICE
AFTER STEERPIKE'S ACCESSION   Barquentine's office post Steerpike.

1·12·98.   (22)

G

Electric Fire in blocked-up fireplace.

Shiny Floor. Grey walls. Window with giant lense, and perhaps flat lenticular glass in the rest. Chrome steel edging. Walls lined with double-height grey filing Cabinets. Steerpike's desk, dark grey 'marble', perhaps with amber corners, or steel. 'G' insignia in amber on dark grey. Small grey steel desks with 1950's calculators and tall steel stools.

above: Designs by Christopher Hobbs for the office of the Master of Ritual, before and after the fire.

right: 'I want that feeling that if you kick it, you stub your toe. You can smell the kitchen. The characters that are in it for all their grotesqueness are real. They don't fly around on wings, there are no trolls and dragons in this story. It is essentially a story of real people with real passions. And there are weird and grotesque people around, not just in Peake's imagination. Look at the nail bombs in Brixton and Soho.' Christopher Hobbs

which had been the model for the three octagonal sets, Gertrude's bedroom, the cat room, and the baptism pavilion. And lying among the debris on his desk was a musical instrument made out of a 1930s' brass ashtray on a stand. It looked like a giant brass oboe, and experts in ancient music advised him where to put in the finger holes.

The only identifiably 'modern' part of the design is the document room, after Barquentine has been killed, and Steerpike, the usurper, has forced his way to the top of the pile. There is an electric fire, and the clean rather fascistic lines of an office. The painting of a piebald horse with a peep-hole cut in it has survived the fire, but to mark the change of time to a more modern era, the horse's hooves have been replaced with wheels!

When Barquentine, the menacing and rather

bullying Keeper of the Ritual, falls burning from the window of this room, taking his tormentor with him, it is the end of an era. The window of the old room, which jutted out over the moat like the nose-cone of a Second World War bomber, has gone, and we are in the control room of a power station. It is not described quite like this in the book, but visually it seems to define the extent of Steerpike's revolution. At the same time as reflecting totalitarian regimes in the 1930s of the right and the left, in Berlin and in Moscow, there is something of Britain at the turn of the century in this Steerpike. It is as if the worst of the old restrictive practices of trade unions have been swept aside in favour of the modernisers of New Labour.

The walls of documents (actually recycled wallpaper catalogues!) have been burnt in the fire, and Steerpike and his smart young men have everything filed away. Although clinical, there is a kind of beauty to the clean lines and uncluttered architectural features of Steerpike's new office. Christopher wanted to make it look beguiling and attractive: 'People are tempted into evil. There are those people who like what Steerpike offers. They like the black uniforms and the rather clean architecture and things. Sweep away the past. Replace it with something clean and new. We have all seen the politicians who love to do that!'

Much of the comedy in Gormenghast exists in this paradoxical universe of darkness and light where bad things are not necessarily ugly.

For the kitchen scenes at the start of Episode One, we tried at first to use rubber meat, but it did not look right, so we sent out for a trailer load of genuine carcasses. We ended up with cows and sheep hanging from the ceiling, and game birds on the kitchen slabs, with real blood and blobs of meat among a slew of cabbage leaves and potato peelings on the floor. After a

Christopher Hobbs in his favourite set – the Library.

All things in the long room absorbed his melancholia. The shadowing galleries brooded with slow anguish; the books receding into the deep corners, tier upon tier, seemed each a separate tragic note in a monumental fugue of volumes.
(*Titus Groan*: 'The Library')

The only way to see whether the books would burn was to set light to them!

few hours under the lights it certainly smelt authentic!

But where we could fake it and still get the required effect, we did so. It all depended on what it looked like on camera. The stone floor slabs throughout the castle are actually made of flooring felt, layered with latex, and cut into shapes of pieces of stone modelled on Nepali or Tibetan floors. It is light and very manoeuvrable, and almost silent, with a comforting dead acoustic. The actors like it, because it is warm and soft underfoot.

We were particularly concerned that the actors should not be overwhelmed by the sets. The aim is that the backgrounds are sparse, needing the presence of the actor to complete the design. The background could be very simple, if there were elements of the set which had authentic beauty. The doorways, furniture and fabrics are real, while some of the surrounding

designs are deceptively simple. Christopher has been working to this principle for many years, developing it on films like *Caravaggio* and *Edward II* with Derek Jarman. For him the textures are the key. The search is always for the right textures to blend in behind the actors, so that the design is not a distraction from the action.

In *Gormenghast* the library, the place where Lord Groan lives in his mind, was Christopher's favourite set. The idea was that it would be like a second-hand bookshop or the library of Trinity College in Dublin, where the volumes appear to go on for ever, a room sculpted out of books. There are quite narrow gaps between the stacks, giving the feeling of being entirely surrounded by books and the smell of books and the look of books – a bibliophile's dream world.

One reference point for authenticity was *The Name of the Rose*, where the books looked like real books. Our background books were very

top: *It is written ... that between these pages where the flax is grey with wisdom, the first-born male-child of the House of Groan shall be lowered and laid lengthways, his head directed to the christening bowl.* (*Titus Groan*: 'Titus is Christened')

above: The Masters' Common Room.

right: The director of photography, Gavin Finney.

exactly like an English public school, with echoes of Oriental influence. It is definably a school in Surrey, yet the desks are made of more timber from the Indian furniture warehouse. As a finishing touch, Christopher carved initials, names and graffiti onto the gnarled surfaces.

When the space was turned into the Common Room, the tobacco-coloured walls were retained, and the air was filled with smoke to match the smoke from a dozen pipes, and a fire in the grate. The masters sat in old leather armchairs, and a stuffed cormorant was nailed to the table with drawing pins. The fisher bird of China was put in as a crucial detail in Peake's description of the room. It is another reference point for readers who know the books, to reassure them that they are in Gormenghast. (The cormorant came from a taxidermist who just happened to have one in his fridge.)

And since the aim is not to recreate Mervyn Peake's Surrey schooldays, but the world of Gormenghast, the view over the trees is a Chinese mountain range. The light shining through the window is not the watery sunshine of England, nor the hot dark sun of America, but the beams of an oriental sun.

When Gavin Finney came on board as the director of photography, he found that the abstract world meant that many normal lighting methods could not be used. If there are no lights visible and no windows to give a clue for light sources, then the director of photography is literally creating another part of the design with the lights and shadows which he throws.

While much of modern film-making uses increasingly naturalistic lighting, because high-quality lightweight cameras make it easier to shoot outdoors, we reached back to the studio movies of the 1940s, when Powell and Pressburger were making films like *Black Narcissus*, *The Red Shoes* and *Stairway to Heaven* on huge sets.

In an early scene Swelter sharpens his

elaborately made, so that they look real and old, and some of them are genuine – for instance, the great book of Groan, which is the centre of the ritual. It was bound properly with immense covers which look like leather, although they were actually cast from the front of an Indian chest, borrowing its ancient textures and detail. All the pages were handwritten and watercoloured in the medieval style with great gilded initial letters, so it was very grand. The aim was to make someone who loves books say, 'I want that.'

When it came to the school in Gormenghast, where Titus is educated, Mervyn Peake describes specific details which we could not do in the film. We ended up with textured tobacco-coloured walls for the Masters' Common Room and the classroom, not the horsehair walls in the book. The two sets were built in the same basic structure, with the aim of making it look and feel

cleaver and prepares to kill Flay, under what
Mervyn Peake describes as 'a lime-green light'.
Gavin found 'the nastiest, most horrible green' he
could and was then left with the problem of
where to put it. Swelter's set was built on a
podium with a big grinder wheel. There was no
window, and no other obvious naturalistic
lighting source as there might have been in a
less abstract castle. But he put his horrible green
gel onto a light and put it *below* Swelter, so his
giant shadow, with the grinder and the cleaver
are thrown up the wall. Then, following film
conventions, Gavin put a little green lantern onto
the set to show where the light was apparently
coming from. But he realised he did not need it,
it just looked silly. So we ended up with
Swelter's grotesque shadow bathed in a green
light which is never explained.

The endless stone lanes of the castle
presented another lighting conundrum. There are
no features other than the texture of the foam
insulation surfaces, and no windows or lamps to
give a clue for lighting sources. As Flay walks

through the corridors of his realm, pursuing or
pursued by Steerpike, the lighting needs to do a
lot of work, promoting the drama of the
situation, otherwise we are left with dull
passageways. Gavin got round the problem by
putting pools of light along the corridor, so the
figures flit in and out of them, and the light
bounces off the columns, sometimes hot on
people's faces, sometimes casting them into
shadows. You are not left thinking that there
should be a light source for these bright pools
along the corridor, but it takes Gormenghast far
away from the candle-drenched tunnels of gothic
fantasy.

The shape of the stone lanes was almost
literally made up as filming progressed. They
were formed from giant slabs of insulated foam
blocks on wheels. The first day we did it, both
Andy and Gavin were perplexed. There was
nothing in the centre of the set except a series of
high foam platforms like children's building
blocks in a giant's playpen. Andy looked puzzled
and said, 'Where are the corridors?' And

Most of these buildings had about them the rough-hewn and oppressive weight of masonry that characterized the main volume of Gormenghast .... one having at its summit an enormous stone carving of a lion's head.
(*Titus Groan*: 'The Library')

particularly to give the castle its sense of awesome scale.

Gormenghast is the mother of all castles, occupying imaginary time and space. When Christopher tried to map it out, using clues in the text, it came out as large as Greater London, and things which should have connected did not! To achieve the overwhelming scale we turned to models, filmed in water. We were sceptical at first, because there has always been an unwritten rule in films that it is hard to do things convincingly underwater. In the past, even submarines were filmed in smoke-filled rooms, not water tanks. But Christopher made a convincing case with a photograph of an eerie mountain kingdom. The city looks as if it could be miles wide. In fact that first prototype model is just three inches tall! It was shot in a small fish-tank in his back garden with cotton wool as clouds, and Dettol swirling around to give some atmosphere. Crucially, this giant illusion cost just a few pence.

Christopher said, 'Wherever you'd like them. Choose your corridor.' By tweaking the blocks to get the view, we found we could create the castle however we wanted. We even discovered how to make curved walls of corridors. It was like working in the most sophisticated Legoland!

But for illusions on the grander scale, we used computer-generated effects. There was a key principle in our use of computers: that they were an extension of our existing designs. Unlike, say, the new *Stars Wars* film, which is a celebration of computer technology, revelling in images spun from software, we used computers only to do things which could not otherwise be done,

Christopher first developed the technique when recreating Dickensian England on *The Wolves of Willoughby Chase*. And he adapted it for Denis Potter's futuristic swansong *Cold Lazarus*. Now the methods are very sophisticated, although the cotton wool and Dettol are still there, even for a model in a 7ft long tank, a leviathan of the miniature world which gives huge flexibility.

In the smallest studio space at Shepperton,

Christopher Hobbs, with one of the key ingredients to make the model work – Dettol.

we built a world as big as Mervyn Peake's imagination, helped by a piece of simple physics: the water appears to magnify the tiny kingdom, so that the glass side of the tank itself acts as an extra lens. That means that everything is made bigger, and it is all in focus because it is brought forward onto the side of the tank. If the light shining into the tank is in the right place, then shadows fall as they would in a real city or forest.

There were three tanks side by side, with the stone forest in one, and the sections of the kingdom of Gormenghast in the others. In the background was the constant hum of a pump, as a wide hose hovered over the tiny town, like a sucker from an alien planet. It was there to clear bubbles or anything else which would spoil the illusion of scale. The models were moved painstakingly into position by an operator wielding what looked like a boat-hook as he lay prostrate on a flat ladder suspended across the top of the tank, while Christopher hung pieces of paper to a contraption like a washing-line at the back to make clouds or mountains. With the tank magnifying and unifying the scene, we gained an impression of great depth, as if the bits of paper and polythene at the back really were a distant mountain range. Outside the tank, and mounted close to the glass in its own black tent to record this microscopic fantasy, sat a 35mm film camera, taking static shots, or tracking to help movement.

In the scene where young Titus escapes from the castle for the first time and wanders bemused through the stone forest on his own, he was first filmed walking slowly in front of a blue screen; then we filmed the stone forest in the tank, with a gentle tracking shot so that the *forest itself* is moving when the two shots are mixed together. Because the eye follows Titus, we believe that he is moving through this enchanted kingdom. The visual effects co-ordinator, Matthew Cope, sat and fretted as he watched the tracking shots, mixing a tape copy of young Titus walking, making sure that the speed and direction were right, on the cheapest video-mixer that money can buy. The real mix was done onto the final transmission tape on the computer back at the Film Factory in Soho.

Some computer techniques have become almost commonplace, although no less magical for that. For example, in the Earling scene on the lake, we needed a crowd of 3,000 or so cheering the ceremony. We had 200 extras applauding on the hillside, and copied them in the computer to fill the gaps. And we added more white cats to swell the tide which follows Gertrude like a train around Gormenghast. We filmed a number of scenes in front of blue screens, allowing other elements to be 'matted' on later by computer. And some scenes are inserted into others, such as the Prunesquallors greeting guests. The whole scene, with the actors moving and talking in

front of a real Georgian door, surrounded by a blue screen, was cut out and put into a space in a model house, built between computer-generated walls which took their texture from the *real* foam insulation walls made at Shepperton. So the computer was pasting together elements which all had their roots in the existing designs.

But sometimes, we found that quite complicated images worked best if they were done with old-fashioned film techniques. At the end of Steerpike's climb from the kitchens to the top of the castle, he looks around him to a blue screen, and the computer fills in the roofs of Gormenghast falling away to infinity. He is in the

Storyboard showing Steerpike's rise from squalor.

clouds, after climbing beyond the natural world, to mythical heights. When he looks down to see Fuchsia, the Romeo and Juliet balcony outside her room is real, but is in fact only four feet above the studio floor. The steep wall which falls away beneath it is an illusion, painted on the studio floor, and the sharp, perpendicular edge of the adjacent tower is a simple piece of wood held in front of the camera. This magic trick of Christopher's has even fooled other designers watching the film!

Throughout we needed to believe that this fantasy world could have a concrete reality. So we limited the use of the computer to things which could not be manufactured in the studio. For the chase scenes through the flooded corridors at the end, the water is real, filling a huge tank at Shepperton. Rain pounds down from several rain machines (soaking actors and crew!), and as the flood waters rise, the lighting changes to a steely blue-grey, saturating the castle with the sadness of the impending disaster.

Water plays a key symbolic role, challenging the ritual and the established order in profound ways as it rises through the castle, engulfing Fuchsia and forcing Titus into his silver canoe, 'slim and silver creature of the waterways', to take decisive action against the usurper at last.

Through the course of the story, it is as if we see the extraordinary towers and chambers of Gormenghast through the eyes of the young Earl. Each room seems vivid with the imagination of childhood, and as the baby grows up, we see him contemplating it with his violet eyes.

Titus's room in the heart of the castle reflects his destiny in fairy-tale fashion. He sleeps in a boat-shaped bed, with echoes of what is to come both in Episode Four and in *Titus Alone*, when he takes to a boat during his escape from Gormenghast to explore the world beyond. An early whimsical idea that he could float off in the boat-bed to do battle turned out to be impracticable! Hanging over the bed is a sword which began life as the snout of a swordfish, and fake elephant tusks which Christopher took on from the makers of *Cleopatra* who were at Shepperton before us. The idea is that although Titus has never been out of the castle, he is a traveller, or at least the descendant of travellers who have brought these things back as they came across them on trade routes. Peake's drawings of Titus seem to portray a boy adventurer, and we have given him the belongings of a young prince poised to roam the world.

above: *It was war, now.
Naked and bloody.*
(*Gormenghast*: ch. 72)

below: **Design by
Christopher Hobbs for
Titus's bedroom. The bed
is shaped like a boat.**
*A world ... of swopped
marbles, birds' eggs,
wooden daggers, secrets
and catapults, midnight
feasts, heroes, deadly
rivalries and desperate
friendships.*
(*Gormenghast*: ch. 4)

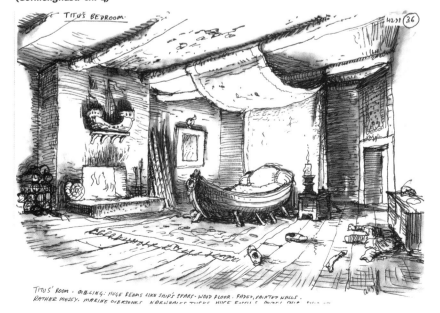

TITUS' ROOM · CEILING: HUGE BEAMS LIKE SHIP'S SPARS· WOOD FLOOR· FADED, PAINTED WALLS.
RATHER MESSY. MARINE OVERTONES. NARNHALES TUSKS. HUGE SHELLS. BIRDS' EGGS. SHIP·

For the final shot of the film, we travelled deep into the mountains in Wales to find a different world. We were in search of a single and crucial image. We needed a wild and eerie vista, a far cry from the fashioned beauty of Gormenghast, to signal Titus's freedom. Christopher remembered a huge standing stone he had chanced upon in a long walk in the Brecon Beacons, and we combed the mountainsides until we found it. The stone, tall, ancient and beautiful, reminded me of Mervyn Peake's observation that somehow Gormenghast was more spiritual than material, and matched perfectly the stone described so powerfully in the final pages of the Trilogy.

We took a small posse up the mountain amongst the sheep to film Titus. First he looked back towards the castle, now a wild horizon, later to be a model shot matted on in the computer. The last glimpse of his childhood and the place which he later calls **'the proof of his sanity and his love'**. Then he looked down the valley from the Great Stone to freedom, and beyond. I watched the white horse, a tiny dot hurtling down the slope taking hedges and ditches, with the knowledge that Titus was to return. **'You'll tread the circle, Titus Groan,'** says Gertrude.

In the final pages of *Titus Alone*, the story beyond the end of our film, Titus comes back to this Great Stone and it seems for a moment, he will turn the corner and return to Gormenghast. The words echoed in my head and in the wind, **'He had no longer any need for home, for he carried his Gormenghast within him. All that he sought was jostling within himself. He had grown up. What a boy had set out to seek a man had found, found by the act of living.**

'There he stood: Titus Groan, and he turned on his heel so that the great boulder was never seen by him ever again.'

Lord Groan

Ian Richardson

These books had great resonance when I first read them, soon after the collapse of Britain's influence as an Empire builder. *Gormenghast* is about corruption, whether it is fascism, or extreme left-wing agitation, that can eat like a cancer into a firmly established state. Steerpike is the rebellious outsider – Hitler, or Milosevic, if you like. His thinking has got to be as brutal as that.

This cast is something I don't think I have ever encountered in my professional life. And this is a British production, not an American one, which means your money is up there on the screen, and not in the pockets of some big American star who gets £5 million a movie. I have always thought that to be the most exciting thing about working for the BBC. You groan a bit because you have got to devote several weeks to accomplishing something, for nothing like the kind of money you would get commercially, but it just looks so fantastic. I think that for the audience coming to it at the Millennium, it has a great deal to say in terms of television excellence on all

fronts. I think it also has something to say about what can be rotten in a state and cause that state just to collapse.

Groan is without question the most complex character I have ever undertaken in my entire professional career, which is forty years this year. Groan is groaning under the weight of the tyranny of protocol and ritual that has remained unbroken like the British Raj for so many years. The library is his world, and when that library is destroyed, his world, his mind is destroyed with it. Because there ain't no love going between that extraordinary wife and him, is there? How they managed at last to get the son, God alone knows! They never even see each other; it must have been a remarkable piece of luck!

When I first took the part, I suggested that it might not be a bad idea to ask if there was any material available on owls that I could look at on video cassette, since the BBC has this Natural History Unit in Bristol. In a week a package arrived in my Devon house full of owls. I found four owl idiosyncrasies and I used

them all, but I am glad my owl acting is over. I had to sink myself into Radox baths night and morning. I was hunched over, and there were quite a lot of physical high jinks which for an old age pensioner is not as easy as it used to be.

In Ian Richardson's long career, his major roles include Montgomery, Sherlock Holmes, Bill Haydon in *Tinker, Tailor, Soldier, Spy*, and Francis Urqhart in *House of Cards*, and *To Play the King*.

Andy Wilson: It seems to me that there are plenty of rituals which seem rather dull to us, that are imposed upon us by our heritage. In Gormenghast, there's a ritualistic life that is supposed to contain the meaning of your life rather than express any kind of individuality. At the end of the twentieth century we clearly saw that most of the religious and political institutions of the nineteenth century had ossified and decayed: a royal family with no place on our television screens any more and wondering at every turn why they do what they do and why we pay for it. There are a lot

of other rituals in English life which somehow lost their appeal and meaning during the century and yet they are still there. Peake seems to be wistfully aware that some rituals, which hurt you on some levels, are what sustain you on other levels.

The characters that he created are iconic – they are archetypes. There is the king, the hero, the boy, the nanny, the mad king, the queen, the disaffected princess. But saying that they are iconic does not mean that they are two-dimensional. I would say it is the most difficult thing in the world to create an iconic character – it's really much more difficult than creating a naturalistic character, because you have to be very certain of your ground.

It is 'Doctor Who' acting. You have to create the fantasy by being completely committed to it. The idea is that you are in a cardboard set of the Tardis and there are these strange saltcellar robots called Daleks coming at you and you are supposed to take completely seriously what you are doing.

right: The ceremony of the Bright Carvings.

opposite: Ian Richardson as Lord Groan.
How could he love this place? He was part of it. He could not imagine a world outside it; and the idea of loving Gormenghast would have shocked him. To have asked him for his feelings for his hereditary home would be like asking a man what his feelings were towards his own hands or his own throat.
(*Titus Groan*: 'Sepulchrave')

Fuchsia

Neve McIntosh

Fuchsia is such a brat at first. A silly little girl in some ways. She's very horrid and she is so nasty to Nannie. But she grows up – not enough – but she does grow up a bit.

Nowadays she wouldn't survive. Girls are so much tougher now, a lot more independent. She tries to be tough but she doesn't have the independence in her spirit to be as tough as she would like to be. That is why she goes around shouting and screaming quite a bit or just crying! And then she ends it all like a tragic heroine in one of her books.

Neve McIntosh played the female lead in *Psychos* for Channel 4, also directed by Andy Wilson.

Sensitive as was her father without his intellect, Fuchsia tosses her black flag of hair, bites at her childish underlip, scowls, laughs, broods, is tender, is intemperate, suspicious, and credulous, all in a day. Her crimson dress inflames grey corridors.
(*Gormenghast*: ch. 2)

Young Titus
Cameron Powrie

I hadn't ridden before doing this, so I had to do a quick bit of learning but it is nothing too hard. No galloping hell for leather – it's not too bad! Titus doesn't really want to be the prince. He wants to explore what the other children are doing outside of Gormenghast, but he has got all these rituals to do. He doesn't really enjoy doing them, so he wants to discover what everyone else does. It has been good fun. It's not just your average period drama!

Cameron Powrie, aged thirteen, is at Whitgift school in Croydon.

Titus the seventy-seventh. Heir to a crumbling summit: to a sea of nettles: to an empire of red rust: to rituals' footprints ankle-deep in stone. (*Gormenghast*: ch. 1)

Older Titus
Andrew Robertson

I did watch Prince William on TV, to see how he stands. I sympathised more than I probably would have done previously! He manages to stand extremely straight and hardly move at all, while smiling and retaining a human way of behaving, despite the fact that there must be incredibly strict codes of behaviour on what he can actually do. It is very odd because I suppose they never really would be free actually to experience anonymity in any way. Titus can come across as in a way having quite a sheltered, privileged, even spoilt upbringing.

Andrew Robertson graduated from Oxford University in 1998.

Titus could no longer bear to think of the life that lay ahead of him with its dead repetitions, its moribund ceremonies. With every day that passed he grew more restless. (*Gormenghast*: ch. 80)

Chapter 5

Passions and Shadows

Sand Films is perhaps the only film company with a tides table in the reception area. We designed and made our costumes there in Rotherhithe, in a warehouse on the Thames, deep among the Dickensian cobbled streets of the old East End. The building is a treasure trove of reference books and pictures, a factory of illusions. There are Gormenghastian surprises around every corner, models or furniture left from one film or another. In the low-ceilinged rooms where clerks once counted in and out the riches of the busiest port in the world, there are now long shelves stuffed with thousands of pictures and designs: a cornucopia of references from Angels, Animals, Architecture, through Birds, Bridges, Buddha, Canterbury, Carpets, and Castles, to Zanzibar, Zoos and Zulus. We were going to need all of them. The costumes would be crucial in defining the feel of Gormenghast – a place that is recognisable while not being identifiable with any particular place or time – somewhere else, but full of people with real human thoughts and feelings. Among the alternative titles which Mervyn Peake had for the Trilogy was 'Passions and Shadows'. We needed to bring the clothes out of the shadows for the passions to have full play on the canvas of *Gormenghast*, and Odile Dicks-Mireaux was the person to do it. Previously she had always worked in the known world. But now, as the costume designer of *Gormenghast*, she had to invent reality – make a world with its own dress-code. She described the task like this: 'I would say it was more like doing an opera than a piece of TV drama. We had to entertain the audience and convince them that this is a completely different world, where they will *enjoy* being taken.'

As Christopher Hobbs scavenged through the history of architecture to make the castle, so Odile searched through dozens of reference books, borrowing fabric from one century and design and shape from another, to clothe the people who would live in Gormenghast. Nothing is invented; it is all real. Every part of every costume has been done somewhere before, but never brought together quite like this. She made an imaginary world, but it was rooted in the real one, with borrowed conventions put together into a coherent whole with its own internal logic. The highly formalised rituals of the castle helped in defining a set of rules for what people would wear. And this applied as much to the servants as to the Groan family themselves. The trap she had to avoid all the time was that too many elements together might tip into pantomime, while too few would make the world look dull. Odile constantly monitored the designs during filming, and she would simplify things if she thought that the costumes were getting in the way of the action.

We wanted everything to look very old, almost as if the costumes were works of art from

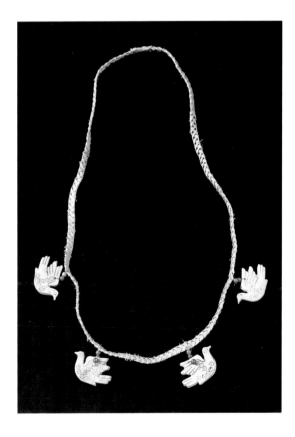

opposite: Detail from Irma Prunesquallor's ballgown.

right: Fuchsia's necklace. *Around her neck are the so-called Daughter's Doves, a necklace of white sandstone doves carved by the 17th Earl of Gormenghast, strung together on a cord of plaited grass.* **(***Titus Groan***: 'The Dark Breakfast')**

The Elizabethan world picture on the Queen's underskirt – an inspiration for Gertrude's dress.

where there is no machinery or mass-production. They don't change very often; they don't have wardrobes full of different clothes. Before Odile could write all the rules which would inform the designs, there were simple but crucial questions to answer, like how cold it was in the castle. And gradually in the Rotherhithe warehouse, as the look emerged, we assembled a team who were making clothes in the way that we imagined they might have been made in Gormenghast.

For Gertrude, a woman of gargantuan scale, we had the image of Wagnerian heroines crossed with Elizabeth I, while always remembering to look to the East of Mervyn Peake's China-fuelled imagination. The first problem was colour. In the book, Gertrude is always dressed in black, but with her long dark red hair, we were worried that she would be too dark. And black tends to make people look thinner on TV, which was not what was wanted for this colossal creature, so we were led by Mervyn Peake's choice of green for her eyes. After giving her green contact lenses, we chose moss green as her defining dress colour, bringing in a colour from the garden for Mother Earth herself. This had an added benefit of accentuating the change when she moves to the black frock of a widow after the death of Lord Groan. Odile picked up a useful device from the Elizabethans, in the way they literally put their world on their clothes. A famous underskirt made for Elizabeth I is covered with animals, and other

a museum. In the book Fuchsia wears an ancient necklace of sandstone doves which was carved by the seventeenth Earl of Gormenghast; Titus wears his father's iron crown, and Odile gave him his father's jacket. The clothing worn by this 'royal family' has been hand-made from hand-dyed fabrics, then passed down through the generations, repaired and looked after in a place

Design by Odile Dicks-Mireaux for Gertrude's dress.

opposite: Detail of Gertrude's dress, with birds.

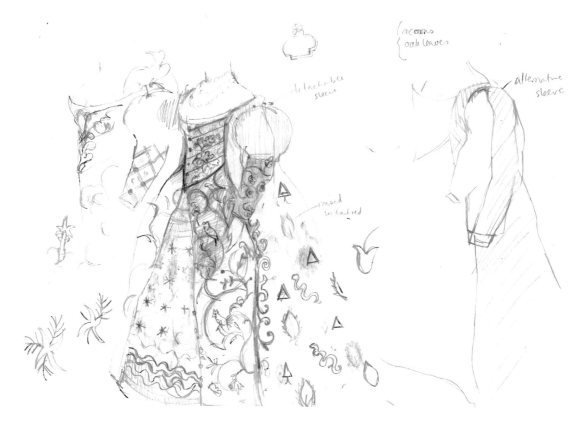

symbols of the world seen from the Elizabethan view. Gertrude's dress, in its turn, is covered with birds and cats, and our invented heraldic symbols of Gormenghast: owls and snails. But to give them a twentieth-century feel the images are bolder and blown up in size.

Much of the power of the costumes comes from details which may not be obvious on the screen. For example, Gertrude's buttons are made from hazelnuts, Swelter's buttons are owls. But it was important that we did not cut corners. When he saw them, Christopher Hobbs said that the costumes looked as if they were made by an 'Italian couturier'. And the shape is determined as much by what is not seen. Celia Imrie had a corset which accentuated her cleavage, and then a chemise, petticoat, and underskirt under the

huge velvet dress. Since other actresses have experienced back problems with this kind of burden, the corset was designed to spread the load like a rucksack. Beneath it, for height, she wore her five-inch 'Spice Girl' shoes (the real thing, bought from the high street for hidden comfort, not this time a copy), and above the corset she had a latex prosthetic, going all the way up to her cheeks, to give her bulk.

Every night, the prosthetics technician David White injected liquid latex into a fibre-glass mould made from Celia's face, and cooked it in the oven. Early every morning, as she sat in Make-up as still as stone for two hours, he stuck the giant neck and face onto Celia with glue, working the edges onto her skin with a sort of elastic paint which would survive for about five hours before the heat worked its way in. On set Celia would sit next to a fan whenever she could, to

right: Detail of owl design on buttons for Swelter.

far right: Ceremonial ring for Lady Groan.

keep the temperature down (and keep off any food or drink that might send her to the loo, since that exercise was an assault course). And whenever the camera was turning on her, David was close by with his glue and his paint, ready to make running repairs. We knew that if anything went wrong with the prosthetic face, then we would probably lose a day's filming. Although David always had a spare, removing the old prosthetic and putting on a new one would have taken up to three hours.

Fuchsia presented different problems. At the start of the story she is 'a girl of about fifteen with long, rather wild black hair'. By the end, she is a woman in her thirties. The difference is achieved by more than just flattening her chest at the start and boosting it at the end. The cut of her dresses, and the choice of the fabrics, defines her age as well. For us she was the

princess painted by Velázquez, with something of the alabaster features of Botticelli's imagination. And of course she is Juliet on her balcony, and Ophelia drowning herself in the lake. Odile saw her as a supremely impractical girl, who would always wear a velvet frock even for a walk in the woods. She said, 'I think if you were living in a world of the royal family, you would not regard these clothes as anything special. You would put on this jewelled frock but not be fussed about it that much.' We made much use of the potential for wearing different layers, with Fuchsia wearing only part of her costume, in different scenes. So she was dressed in softer skirts in her own room, putting on the big dress when she went outside.

The main dress worn by the young Fuchsia is made of red velvet covered with stars. But when she is older, the fabric is much more complicated, made of four layers in all. The base is just a

As for Fuchsia, it was all so new and tremendous to her that her emotions had enough on which to feed. She was happier than she had ever been in her life. (Gormenghast: ch. 53)

Neve McIntosh as Fuchsia
– teenage Princess.

right and opposite: 'I have
to wear hefty dresses for
this. My later ones are big
corset jobs with big skirts
and they are very heavy.
You only notice it when it
comes off and you feel
you rise an inch or two,
just because of the weight
of all this material.'
Neve McIntosh

Elisabeth de Valois
(1081–1131). Inspiration
from the beginning of the
last millennium for
Fuchsia's collar.

terracotta-coloured winceyette, and then the
other layers are built on top of that, including
bits of a 1910 dress bought in an auction, which
has the sheen of a pearlised finish. We cut it up
and stitched it on, as if it were hand-
embroidered.

Although the hand-made cut of the costumes
was supposed to replicate the cottage-industry
feel of Gormenghast itself, preparing the fabrics
involved baser arts. One day I arrived at
Rotherhithe to find an assistant pointing a blow-
torch at Gertrude's dress! The scorching put a
couple of centuries onto the age of the fabric,
and it never mattered if the clothes picked up
dust, since that gave them authenticity as items
which were worn around the castle. But the water
gave us more of a problem, turning costume-
maintenance into a full-time job. Fuchsia falls off
a cliff in the rain in Episode Three, and throws
herself into the water in Episode Four, dressed
impractically as usual as a princess. Odile knew
that apart from the obvious budgetary
considerations, these costumes were unique
works of art in themselves, and it would be hard
to motivate the team to copy them. For the few
costumes which she could not avoid copying, she
had to be careful how she asked for the work to
be done: 'You have to be sensitive to your
costume-maker, very sensitive. So we wouldn't

Detail of Fuchsia's collar.

June Brown as Nannie
Slagg.
*'Another baby, after all
this time! Oh, I could
smack him already.'*
(*Titus Groan*:
'Prunesquallor's Knee-cap')

above left: Spanish gypsy
inspiration from 1930s for
Nannie Slagg's hat.

right: Design by Odile
Dicks-Mireaux for the
twins' dresses.

far right: Fabric for the
twins' dresses.

'It is as though their brains tick at the same time. They become bewildered by anything they don't quite understand. They have sat in the South Wing for thirteen years thinking, but it is really arduous exercise for them. We have three hours in Make-up and the character slowly develops as we put everything on. We become united during that time. And we find that when we run through lines, the voice is there. We try and make our eyebrows similar, because eyebrows very much determine a character. And we have to change the shape of our lips.' Lynsey Baxter as Cora.

'They are half of the same person. Mervyn Peake described their voices as flat as haddocks. We worked on the premise that they were childlike in many ways. Then we found a flattish tone that was irritating as well as boring. We had also to develop certain mannerisms which were peculiar to them, which unified them. We developed a thing instinctively together, where we would twiddle with something or we had a particular mannerism. It was quite hard to do, but I think it unifies them. It makes them strange. They totally believe that they have been done out of their true role in life.' Zoë Wanamaker as Clarice.

opposite: Detail of the twins' dresses.

mention it for a long time until things were calm. Then I would say, "Just by the way, we've got to make ... !"'

Like the dresses of the other members of the Groan family, the fabric for the gowns worn by the twins cost only about £20 a piece. The base is a corduroy, bought, as almost all of the fabrics were, amid the bustle of Brick Lane market, on the other side of the river from the Rotherhithe warehouse. The purple (a royal colour) shines through the upper layers, hand-stitched pieces of cloth, under a cheap gold lamé netting on the outside.

The twins' make-up presented a formidable challenge. They need to look so similar that, in Mervyn Peake's words, they are 'identical to the point of indecency'. Sandra Shepherd, who did their make-up every day, said that she concentrated on three things to turn Zoë Wanamaker and Lynsey Baxter into twins: their

Design by Odile Dicks-Mireaux for Lord Groan's ceremonial cape.

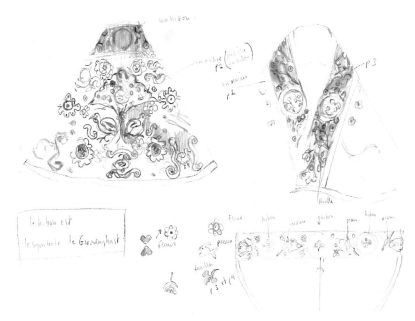

Lord Groan's cape.

above: Matador influence for Steerpike's costume as a servant in the Prunesquallor household.

right: *'You do interest me, I must admit that much, Master Steerpike ... or rather you tantalize me in a pleasant sort of way.'* Dr Prunesquallor (*Titus Groan*: 'At the Prunesquallors')

eyebrows, the slant of their eyes and their lips. For equality, she copied one mole from Lynsey's face, and one from Zoë's, while the hairdresser Liz Michie fitted the wigs, after shaving Zoë's hairline at the front. It helped that the twins are supposed to have both suffered from something like a stroke at the same time, both losing the use of their left hands. So their make-up is daubed on in big blobs of colour, as if put on by a child.

Nannie Slagg is in a dark grey 'uniform', and we built a little hump in the back at June Brown's request. It is almost indiscernible, but it gave her the right look as she bustles about, complaining about her heart.

For the men, Odile's starting point was a book of photographs taken in Hungary at the end of the nineteenth century. Hungary's isolated aristocracy, in the dying days of an empire which had straddled east and west, reminded her of Gormenghast. The pictures infused the designs with a fading *fin de siècle* grandeur which was not specifically English. But Odile did not stay in Hungary. Again, the key was to find a mix, which

right: Steerpike – injured, but at the summit of his powers, and wearing the Royal Gormenghast owl. *The burns on his face and neck were there to stay ... His mind, always compassionless, was now an icicle – sharp, lucent and frigid. From now onwards he had no other purpose than to hold the castle ever more tightly in the scalded palm of his hand.* (*Gormenghast*: ch. 46)

far right: Detail of owl claws on Lord Groan's dressing gown.

right: Detail of Barquentine's costume.

far right: Detail of Lord Groan's coat.

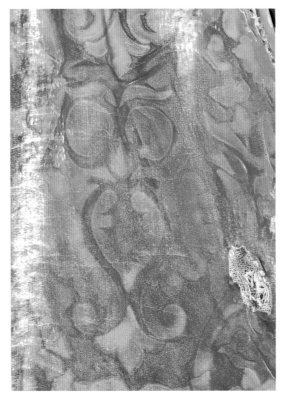

did not define or limit Mervyn Peake's castle. So although the formal but exotic Hungarian court gave early inspiration, the Elizabethan age lent shape. In Gormenghast, court clothes were topped by an oriental collar, like the collar on a Nehru suit, while the body-shape was sixteenth century.

Odile needed to enter the world of the court, making rules for the rituals, so that when a

character faced a situation, she would know what costume to choose. Lord Groan is most often seen in the interminable rituals which punctuated his life, and Odile gave him a cape made from latex, moulded and sculpted to look like leather, and covered with the Gormenghast heraldic symbols, the owl and the snail, woven into an intricate pattern with other quasi-religious motifs. Ian Richardson made maximum dramatic use of

above left: Seventeenth-century English design which inspired Lord Groan's nightshirt.

above right: Detail of sleeve of Lord Groan's nightshirt.

right: Ian Richardson, wearing contact lenses to give him the eyes of an owl.
'Be quiet now. Hush, then, and do your will ... Great wings shall come, great silent, silent wings ... Goodbye. All's one. All's one. All's one.'
(*Titus Groan*: 'Blood at Midnight')

the cape when he turned into an owl, running along and flapping it like a pair of wings.

After Lord Groan's death, young Titus borrows some of his clothes, and not only because of their ritual significance. This device seemed to suit Gormenghast, with the authenticity of the aristocracy who will mend and make do, rather than buy new.

In contrast, Steerpike has many clothes. One of the first things which Irma says after he works his way into the Prunesquallor household is, 'We shall dress him in pale grey', and so he is. The cut is Elizabethan again, and he wears a short little jacket, based on a picture of a matador. Johnny's personal style is loose and informal, and Odile tried not to restrict his natural physicality. Then by the time he has risen to Master of the Ritual, his clothes are darker, with a distinct Nazi edge.

On the other hand, the other two key castle servants, Flay and Barquentine, need to look as if they have not changed for hundreds of years. Barquentine's rags are made of velvet designed to look as if it has been worn since the Renaissance, and Flay's long dark clothes make him thin and ageless. Odile had a curious

problem with Christopher Lee, in that although he is in his seventies, he does not look it. He is not a decrepit servant, but has the statuesque bearing of a man half his age.

The length of his coat, and his curious half-sleeves are inspired by those Hungarian court pictures. He is the senior servant, and looks distinctive, but the same look is repeated in part for the livery of other castle servants, who were then topped off with *purple* wigs, putting them firmly in the fantasy world of Gormenghast.

Odile's magpie instincts continued down the line. The castle rituals are witnessed by men who look like coptic bishops, in Tibetan hats, with choirboys in hessian robes. And the birth of Titus is presided over by nurses who flutter to and fro in giant head-dresses like Breton peasants.

The approach reaches its eclectic conclusion in the outfits we made for the teachers. They are made of woollen tweed fabric, as if from Edwardian England. But they have sleeves and giant pockets from the Hungarian court, and the cut is the same narrow sixteenth-century shape which proved to be so flexible throughout.

At the other extreme from the teachers, who live in the core of the castle, are the Bright

opposite: *'My ceremonial velvet, Flay. Be as quick as you can. My velvet and the bird-brooch of opals.'* (*Titus Groan*: 'A Bloody Cheekbone')

below: 'We are members of a chorus, with individual characters, who react to events as one man.'
Martin Clunes
From left: Phil Cornwell, James Dreyfus, Martin Clunes, Mark Williams, Steve Pemberton.

The land dipped gradually to the water and on this decline was gathered what was pleased to think itself the upper stratum of Gormenghast society. (*Gormenghast*: ch. 50)

right: The Bright Carvers
Their children had radiance, their eyes, the sheen on their hair, and in another way, their movements and their voices. Bright with a kind of unnatural brightness. (*Titus Groan*: 'Mrs Slagg by Moonlight')

far right: Spanish gypsy reference which inspired the look of the Bright Carvers' wives.

Carvers who live outside. In the film, they represent a different way of living, a world of freedom and creativity, and it was crucial that we found a look which celebrated that. Odile found this one of the hardest challenges. There are few clues in the book as to what Mervyn Peake thought they looked like, as Odile noticed: 'In the book you get the brightness through their eyes, which is a really difficult thing to do on screen!' The other problem was that there were a lot of them. In one scene 150 extras came to play the Carvers. The solution was to get old stock from a number of different ethnic places and periods – Spain, North Africa, Russia, Tibet – and then use a few simple devices to unify the whole. Many of the men wore sashes, and since they were working craftsmen, they wore leather aprons.

Although they are 'outsiders', the Carvers are not part of any identifiable time or place. They are still part of the imaginary vision, bound into the ritual of the castle, living on its benificence. So the trick in designing the costumes and those of the whole 'world' of Gormenghast was to draw together dozens of elements and inspirations, into a look which can be recognised as itself and nowhere else. In the fragments of the libretto for a Gormenghast opera which Mervyn Peake planned to write with Benjamin Britten, he defined its timeless harmony:

> **'In a place no atlas will help you to discover**
> **At a time that doesn't matter**
> **For nothing changes, though the hands**
> **Go round and around, and the bells clang.'**

Gertrude
Celia Imrie

Celia Imrie as Gertrude. *His mother, half asleep and half aware: with the awareness of anger, the detachment of trance. She saw him seven times in seven years ... Her love for him is as heavy and formless as loam. A furlong of white cats trails after her ... She is the Countess Gertrude of huge clay.*
(*Gormenghast*: ch. 2)

It has everything: wild birds, children, lots of cats, side-saddle, false teeth, contact lenses, Spice Girl shoes, a huge costume – and a new neck. My earliest start was a 4.15 pick up to be here for 5 o'clock. But I can't do very much. I can't put my own wig on, I can't put my own prosthetic on. And once the contact lenses are in it is quite difficult to read. So I have to sit here. It is

a miracle that he stays on my shoulder. My heart is in my mouth every time. He is nearly *insolent*, the way he looks at everybody, which is of course perfect because Gertrude thinks herself that everybody yacks on far too much. And he has only pecked me twice, but luckily I have got a false face, so it has been more trouble for Dave (the prosthetics craftsman) than for me. It is

inside, but on the other hand it is quite good for me to look at myself as I am because then I have got to be as big as she is. I have got to wander around the doors and the corridors as if I do it all my life. And I get to ride side-saddle, which I think is so elegant – I don't actually see the point of being on a horse unless there is a film crew around, because it is all so

probably quite a good thing because Gertrude is a very calm person, which I am not necessarily. Andy keeps saying 'the less you do, the more powerful it is'. A lot of Gertrude has to be *underneath*, I suppose. She is excruciatingly unmaternal, but her expression gives away nothing. You have no idea what she is thinking – she behaves in a more protective tigressy way when her cat is hurt than when her son is.

She does know from quite early on that there is something wrong. And I think that if she and Steerpike were able to confess, they would both have quite a lot of admiration for each other. There is a wonderful line where he says, 'I am the son you should have had.'

It is an extraordinary relationship that Jimmy and I have built up. I think it is

My Spice Girl shoes are one of the most comfortable things I have got, surprisingly. They make me feel very tiny

romantic. But when I do it on camera, I have to make it *look* as if I do it every single day of my life.

Celia Imrie has starred in films from *Star Wars* to *The Borrowers* and *Hilary and Jackie*, and performed TV comedy with Victoria Wood and Julie Walters.

Andy Wilson: Gertrude is this gigantic woman who obliterates furniture and has hundreds of cats. When Celia was told in a scene of Fuchsia's death, she was able – even against all the emotionless disaffection that is built into the character of Gertrude – to let one tear roll down her cheek. It was profoundly moving, speaking volumes about everything Gertrude had ever done and said to and for her daughter. If she had been an *Alice in Wonderland*-style Red Queen, it would not have happened. I love Lewis Carroll as well, but his intention was not to create something like Gormenghast. You couldn't get to the end of *Alice in Wonderland* and say, 'Right. Something has happened. Now cry!' In Gormenghast, we are dealing with real people in a world of fantastic reality.

Gertrude is not cruel, she is dispassionate. She knows she has to fulfil a function and she doesn't rebel against her lot. And if you want to look for it, the analogy with our own Queen is there. As everything tumbles around her she stays calm. She has to stay calm. She can go on television and say, 'I've had the most awful year', in a dispassionate way, whereas any normal human being having had that year might break down in front of the camera. The Queen is not allowed to do that. So the single tear rolling down the cheek was perfect. Absolutely what it should be.

Richard Griffiths (Swelter) describes the opening of the film:

'At the beginning, you are looking at a tropical landscape. It is red and pink and black – like looking though a glass darkly at lost armies fighting. But it resolves itself into an image of a valley seen from a great height. You realise that it is a distant view of the Rift Valley, the gigantic, torturous valley that cuts across Africa. The camera-shot pulls back, and you realise that you weren't looking at a landscape at all. What you were actually looking at was an eye.

And it pulls back a bit more and the eye itself is what is pink and red, because it is an albino eye. It is not a human eye; it's the eye of a white rook called Master Chalk. And the camera pulls back and reveals this bird beating along, over the Rift Valley. The camera comes round behind the bird, and we follow this improbably beautiful white bird as he flies through; and it is not the Rift Valley any more; it's the Grand Canyon; it's not the Grand Canyon; it turns into the Himalayas and it goes up and it gets higher and higher and higher. The valley gets narrower and deeper into gorges, while the mountains rear up in the background. And there in the distance it is like Tibet and you see this city of Lhasa.

He flies up ever higher and it's not a city any more, it is revealed as a gigantic fortress, the castle of Gormenghast which is actually in a sort of England. He flies up and through it and when he gets close to the castle, you realise that the walls are rearing up thousands of feet high. He somehow gets through that. He is flying along between the buildings which themselves are bigger than a vehicle assembly building in Texas. And he

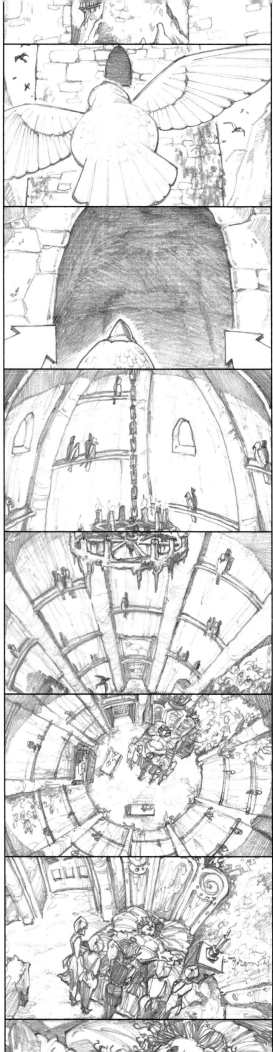

is still getting higher and higher. There are lights twinkling in the night because the light is falling all the time, and the bird comes above the rooftops. The rooftops go for miles in all directions but he knows his way and he flies along a line. He comes to this gigantic turret and flies up it and there are hundreds of people inside the rooms of this turret and they are all concerned and worried and all their attention is moving up to where the bird is flying. He goes through a window at the top and he lands, and he is in the Countess's bedroom, and she is giving birth to Titus.'

'I had no idea how heavy a baby is. It is like a wriggling little puppy, a very powerful little thing. I really had to hold on to it, with a firm grip on head and bum like a rugby ball. The baby's real mother was standing there and I thought to myself "If you drop this kid ... !"'
John Sessions

Chapter 6

'Get Me That Rook!'

One of the undoubted stars of *Gormenghast* is not a person, although he is an actor, since he has spent all of his short life being trained to do just this. He is a white crow, less than two years old, who is rather inevitably called Jimmy White, after the snooker player. He was one of the first stars we lined up for the show, during 1998, when we were spending money that we did not know we had, preparing for a show which we did not know would be approved, during long months of putting the whole package together.

We had been agonising about the white rook. We could certainly not leave him out; he plays a vital role as almost the only being who Gertrude has a real relationship with. We had gloomily gathered estimates for animated birds which were well beyond our budget, knowing that even the best animation in the world was not going to have the authenticity we wanted. Then one day Andy Wilson picked up a copy of the *Daily Telegraph* in the foyer of Channel Four television, while he was waiting for a meeting, and read a short news story about this white bird which had been found in a field in West Wales. It was a moment of such serendipity that he could not let it go. He later told me that this was the moment when he really believed we would make the film. With the instincts of a Hollywood mogul, he ordered, 'Get me that Rook!'

Genuine albino crows (or rooks, we thought Mervyn Peake would forgive us this slight species change!) are very, very rare. Jimmy is believed to be the only one alive in Britain. He had been found by a boy out walking, and he was already being attacked by other birds. Steve Harty, the manager of the Aberaeron Wildlife Park, where he ended up, has no illusions about the cruelty of nature. 'He was only about three weeks old. The parents must have decided they weren't going to look after him any more so they pushed him out of the nest. Of course, if anything is white it is odd, so other things go for it. It is a bit like

human beings, if they find something odd, the first thing they want to do is kill it.'

That explains why the bird is so rare. The albino gene is fairly common in some birds. Steve used to have a breeding colony of albino blackbirds himself. But the ruthless policy of racial purity practised in the wild means that genuine albino crows never survive.

When he first came, he was very thin and weak, and had been badly pecked. For the first few days Steve kept him in his bedroom, and fed him every two hours, night and day.

The intensity of this hand-rearing means that Jimmy could never be returned to the wild, like some other birds which Steve has nursed back to health. But there was still a lot of work to do before he could do what was needed amid all the distractions of a studio. It is a big space, and apart from anything else, we needed to know that he would not just fly up and disappear in the giant roof space, among the metal gantries

opposite: *In her deep voice she would hold converse with him for an hour at a time, referring to him as 'Master Chalk' or her 'wicked one'.* (*Titus Groan*: 'While the Old Nurse Dozes')

right: Steve Harty, the Birdman, with Jimmy.

and walkways, or hurt himself on the lights. We needed him to sit for hour after hour, under hot lights, on the right shoulder of Gertrude, Countess of Groan, played by Celia Imrie.

Steve had done some film work before. When *The Lion King* opened, he took a lion cub around a number of cinemas to be photographed, and less riskily, he did a promotional tour with a red deer, when *Bambi* was re-issued. But he had never done a long shoot with just one bird before. Any animal trainer would want the comfort of a double as an insurance policy – for the making of *Babe,* they got through a lot of pigs – but we had *the* only white crow there was, so nothing could go wrong. We did use a model bird for some long shots, and in many respects it looked very impressive. But it never had anything like the awesome animal power of the real Jimmy.

When he started the training for real, the only actor Steve knew we were going to have was Warren Mitchell, so he set up a TV in the cage, and he would play old *Till Death Us Do Part* videos, gradually turning up the volume! The ruse paid off. In an early scene, Jimmy was sitting on Gertrude's shoulder when Barquentine, played by Warren Mitchell, clumped up on his grotesque crutch, coming as close as he could to her face, and then shouting at Gertrude from only a few inches away. Jimmy just sat there and watched unconcerned, through several takes. He had heard Alf Garnett screaming for long enough in his cage, this was no different! Steve is convinced that Jimmy really did recognise the voice: 'He is very clever. Crows, rooks and jackdaws are all part of the *corvidae* family, and they are among the most intelligent birds you will come across. They recognise sounds and voices.'

The first few days that Jimmy was on set, we were wary of how much he would be able to do, but he exceeded expectations, and surprised us with his versatility. At the beginning, he would fly off Celia's shoulder at the smallest noise or the movement of a boom microphone. But by the end, his flights had become part of the action.

Steve always wore the same dark clothes, so that the bird would recognise him instantly on the set, because he believed that food was not the only trigger to get Jimmy to perform. There was food around of course, and Jimmy had a giant appetite. During interior scenes, when Gertrude would sit for long periods berating somebody, usually Prunesquallor, Jimmy would sit on the back of the sofa, pecking at worms scattered along it. His habit of eating only a few

helped, because it meant that he would still be hungry for the next take, or the tight shot, on the scene. Steve says that crows are different from parrots: 'If you give a parrot a bowl of food, it will sit with it, and go through the whole lot, either throwing it all out on the floor to find the bits that it wants, or it will just eat the whole lot, gone. But even if crows are starving hungry, they might take only two or three bits out of a bowl, and then go and see if there is a worm over in the corner, although there most probably isn't.' That characteristic had the big advantage that we were not filming a bird who was scoffing away. He looked alert, as if he was listening to the scene. But the down side of this inquisitive nature is that Steve was constantly wondering if Jimmy was about to stray off to the imaginary worm in the corner. It was a psychological game: 'It is very difficult to get him to stay in one place. So if I see him starting to look round, I try to break his concentration. He is thinking to himself he wants to get off, for whatever reason. I catch his eye, and I might move my hand or stand in a certain position, because I think he is going to go there, then he sits upright. Or if I can get on and give him a meal worm, then in that split second his concentration is broken, and he forgets that he wanted to fly away. You have got to be bird-brained yourself!'

Between takes, Jimmy would retire to a forty-foot portakabin, which was his temporary home at Shepperton. Sometimes Steve would bring a tame parrot, a jackdaw or a cockatoo from home to keep him company. Like any real star there had been a certain amount of negotiation on living conditions! Originally Jimmy had an aviary built at the side of the prop room. But on the first day, Steve came back after lunch to find fumes from a laminating process next door were coming through. He remembers being very worried: 'I said it had to be moved. It was not a question of moving it today or tomorrow, it had to be done straightaway. The fumes could have killed the bird. So they opened up the big shutter doors and put the fans on to clear the fumes out and within about an hour they had sorted out a portakabin for him. It meant that he had lots of space to fly around.'

The other key part of the equation was Celia Imrie. As far as Steve was concerned this was half of his job. He recalls driving down in some trepidation to meet her for the first time: 'First I brought out a parrot, who is as bomb-proof as you are ever going to get a bird. I had it on Celia's shoulder, just to see how she would react.

'So you beg my pardon, do you? said Lady Groan, 'and you think that's the end of it? No more questions about where you've been or where you've flown these three long weeks? So that's it, is it, Master Chalk? You want me to forgive you for old sake's sake? Come here with your old beak and rub it on my arm. Come along my whitest one, come along, then.' (*Titus Groan*: 'Tallow and Birdseed')

I wasn't so much worried about what Jimmy would do; I was worried about what Celia would do. Some people, although they might have got the part, might be terrified of birds. But it was obvious that Celia was not frightened. So after about twenty minutes of having the other bird out, I let Jimmy out. After they took some still pictures of Jimmy on her shoulder, some other girls came in, and they were all sitting on the floor playing with Jimmy, who was starting to pull at material and play with them. We went out and left Celia with the bird, and about half an hour later we went back in. The lasting memory I've got of Celia was that she was on all fours talking to Jimmy!

'Once the bird went up to Celia's dressing room, and he trashed it unfortunately. He messed on the settee and then he decided he wanted to put a hole in the picture on the wall. He started to shred a bouquet of flowers, landing in the middle of it and knocking the vase of water over. A gallon of water went all over the table and onto the floor. Then he started pulling everything out of her bag. But Celia was just not worried about it, she is so cool and calm. You have to move very slowly around them. If he does peck, the worst thing you can do is to jump because you frighten him.'

Jimmy pecked Celia only twice, but fortunately her thick latex prosthetic took the impact. It was a reminder that he was a wild bird, who could end up anywhere, not necessarily going for the right shoulder. During a banquet, he lost his bearings a bit, and flew onto Fiona

Shaw's head. To her credit, she just sat there while Steve tried to grab him, but he carried on round, landing on Lynsey Baxter as well.

Apart from her friendship with birds, Gertrude was also surrounded by white cats. Since he spends his life with other animals and birds, Jimmy does not have the natural antennae which would warn him of danger. In some scenes, when there were lots of cats around, Steve told us that if Jimmy hopped onto the floor, he would go in and rescue the bird, even if it meant ruining the shot. He was not concerned about most of the cats, since, as he put it: 'Persians are not the greatest hunters in the world.' But he kept a good eye on one particular young cat, which Celia would usually have to hold because he was restless. So in the middle of scenes when we were concentrating on the action, Steve was watching nature in tooth and claw, as Celia clutched her cat, who was eyeing up the crow only feet away on the back of the chair.

The cats and all the other animals were brought in by a specialist animal trainer for films, Sue Clark. The white cats came together from different homes only eight weeks before the show, so they needed to get to know each other, and then her.

In one scene, Flay picks up a cat and throws it across the room at Steerpike (it is the cause of Flay's banishment from the castle). Sue put on Christopher Lee's dark coat, to double as Flay. We see him/her appearing to throw the cat (although she does not let go!), then the cat sat on the 'dolly', the truck under the camera, and whizzed across the room, then we cut to a dummy cat hitting the wall and falling, and then to the real cat rolling out of shot. It was not the only stunt which Sue had to improvise. She produced a monkey, which has its tail cut off, victim of a giant axe which the twins set as a trap for Steerpike.

Sometimes arriving at K Stage in Shepperton was like going to a zoo. There were horses, cattle, sheep baaing from their pens, a monkey, lots of birds, and there was Eric Sykes's goat. He was a two-year-old Angorra with long and rather fearful horns which everyone kept at some distance.

But some parts of Peake's imaginative vision could not be filmed with real animals, and where we could not train them to do what was needed, we turned again to computers. It was obviously not practical to set up the death of Lord Groan for real. He falls, pecked and scratched by a swirling cloud of owls, after believing that he has

right: Storyboards of the death of Lord Groan.

far right, above: Building up the Gormenghast owl inside the computer.

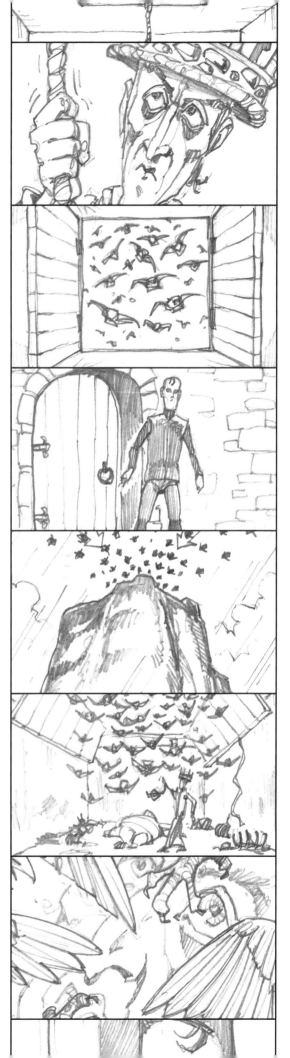

right: Storyboards of the death of Lord Groan.

far right, above: Building up the Gormenghast owl inside the computer.

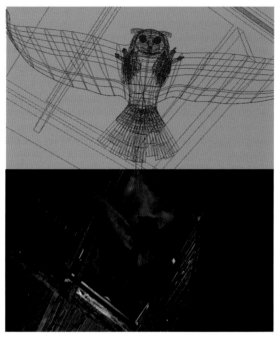

turned into an owl himself. The whole thing was contrived in the computer. All that Ian had to do was to walk up the staircase, open a trap-door, looking up to a blue screen, and act his death-throes. Meanwhile, in the Film Factory in Soho, Simon Giles and his team worked on the owls for months, starting with film of owls which they shot themselves, and some BBC Natural History films, and then finding owls on the Internet, or in books. They were looking for texture as well as shape, and built a prototype Gormenghast owl out of feathers, stitched and glued together onto a wire frame. This was not a cuddly little owl, but a giant, with fearsome claws and a beak, and a wide wing-span. The image was fed into the computer, and then it was replicated thirty or so times, so that when Ian opens the trap-door, a black cloud of owls seems to tumble over and over in the void beyond, and half a dozen break through to encircle his body as he falls. The key to success – turning this illusion into frightening reality – is putting in convincing shadows and depth. New computer tools like 'Henry', and his friend 'Inferno', made all the difference, giving a real 3D feel so you can't see the join.

For the visual effects team, the most difficult scene to achieve was the opening shot of the whole series, where the rook swoops down across the castle, finally resting in Lady Groan's bedroom window. For an afternoon, Jimmy White was encouraged to fly around the studio, after months of being trained to sit still. And once we had all these apparently random shots, we could only hope that one of the soaring dives in front of a blue screen would cut with the real

The sky about the tower became white with the lit bodies of circling owls, and the entrance to the Tower filled with a great weight of feathers, beaks and talons as the devouring of the two incongruous remains proceeded.
(***Titus Groan**: 'Gone'*)

geography of the castle in the water tank, as we tried to follow the swooping moves using the camera mounted in front of the model. The shot was a crucial one, as the flight of the bird takes the camera (and the viewer) into Gormenghast for the first time. It stretched our resources to the limit – the only known albino crow in Britain, made to fly as if across a giant kingdom, which was in reality built in a small tank: all stitched together on the computer in Soho.

The day of encouraging Jimmy White to fly around the studio had consequences for Steve afterwards, who needed to work on persuading him that all we really wanted him to do for nearly all of the time was to sit on Gertrude's shoulder. By chance, the next day's filming was in the most alien environment for him. Gertrude was on the balcony overlooking a ceremony in the Grand Courtyard, so there was a lot of space around Jimmy, and there was a fan set on the ground behind him, to give the illusion of a slight breeze.

If you were to design a scenario in which the crow was meant to take off, then putting him high up, next to an open space, with air blowing up behind him, would be a good way to do it! Jimmy's natural instinct was to take off, or turn around into the breeze. But he managed to stay on the balcony for most of the time, although he left the wide-shot to his wire-and-feathers double.

We knew that every day that Jimmy White did what was wanted was a minor miracle. As his handler Steve said, 'You just can't tell. It is a bird. You don't know what goes on in their tiny minds. Tomorrow he might just think, "I have had enough today and I don't want to play."'

But, luckily for us, that day never came.

Barquentine
Warren Mitchell

Barquentine is a one-legged thing who smites his way through ill-lit corridors on a grim and echoing crutch.
(*Gormenghast*: ch. 2)

I had one big choice to make in the early days. Do I have a leg strapped up or not? I tried being a dwarf, with a leg strapped up, but I kept falling over. So there we were. I sort of stoop a great deal, on crutches, which make me very short.

I find it difficult to talk about Barquentine because he is monochrome and rightly so. To say he is not a nice man would be the understatement of the year. He has no redeeming features whatsoever. I think I can say that it helps me to enhance my reputation as being thoroughly unpleasant: type-cast as a cantankerous old man.

We all operate under what I can only call Peakian logic, Peakian philosophies. I think they must all be a bit bonkers. Take a character like the Countess who is wonderfully objective about everything. It amazes me that she doesn't turn around and say, 'Shut up, you silly old dwarf fart.' But she doesn't. When I say we have got to do this, we have got to have a 'Rafting', she doesn't say, 'A Rafting? You can go and raft yourself!' She could

have done. But she doesn't.

It is very bold TV. I can hear a lot of people saying, 'Did you see that thing last night? I don't know what it's on about. Did you? Did you see it? There was what's his name, the one who is in er ... er ... And the other fella, and that girl, she was in it and all. Funny though, they all talk very funny in it. What's his name – used to swear on the television, he's in it. He's got a beard down to his navel. It didn't fool me. I knew who it was.' That's the sort of thing that you can hear, can't you? After *Gormenghast*.

Warren Mitchell has been a film and TV actor for more than forty years, most famously as Alf Garnett in *Till Death Us Do Part*.

Andy Wilson: Warren Mitchell came with lots of very good, precise ideas about how he wanted to do it – he wanted to be a dwarf, he wanted to be a rabbi, he had based his character on people he knew, and so on. And it was all great. We were doing a scene where Barquentine wakes up and Steerpike is just behind the double doors, and Barquentine goes, 'How is it that you know that I am going to get up every morning?' And on the first few takes Warren kind of naturalised it, and said, 'How is it that you know that I am going to get up every morning?' and it was just like, you know, not a very good line. So I kept pushing him to be more and more, bigger and bigger, and I just kept saying, 'More, bigger, more, bigger, more, bigger!' and finally this enormous scream of 'Damn you, Steerpike! How do you know when I'm going to get up every morning?' at the top of his voice. And then he stared into the camera and said, 'How's that for over-acting, Andy?' and from that point on he was just Barquentine; he was huge the whole time. Which is not to say that he didn't bring some subtlety into it. He did a wonderful scene, where he is talking to Gertrude about Lord Groan having gone missing, where he put this wonderful deep structure into it. But, on the surface, he was the grumpiest man in the world. Iconically he had to be 'the grumpiest man in the world' – the person who is the warden of something like Gormenghast obviously would be, because everything would seem to be going out of control the whole time. That's what I wanted – that iconic performance, and once he had got that, he put the detail in.

June Brown

When they cast me for *Gormenghast*, I said, 'You must be mad.' I kept telling them I was wrong for this, and I suggested other actresses. When are they going to let me play something lovely? I think I am going to have a face lift. When I leave *EastEnders* I'll have a quick tuck here on the side. But I have never done anything like this before. I don't really know what I'm doing. I'm a dress and a wig and a hat, I am, and a pair of mittens, and occasionally an umbrella! Our lovely director, Andy Wilson, calls it high comedy, and I call it comic *grand guignol* because we all get killed. It's not black comedy. It's bigger than that. It's on its own, isn't it?

I can *ad lib* as Dot very easily, but I think they might spot it if I *ad lib* with Nannie Slagg! One is rather careful about this text, because it is so precise. Nannie Slagg feels like a real person to me. She gets quite cross with Fuchsia, but that is the way you are with children you are very close to, you are not necessarily an aunty figure. Basically Nannie Slagg adores the children but I think she has been a nannie for years. She was Lord Groan's nannie. But Gertrude frightens her to death.

The hardest thing I had to do was when she goes out of the castle to the Bright Carvers. Don't they sound lovely, the 'Bright Carvers'? I think Nannie Slagg is quite intimidated by these silent people.

They are very strange and odd. She wasn't born down there, she was born somewhere in the attics of Gormenghast. When she meets them, there are loads of 'ums' in the text. Now I'm not a natural 'ummer' (I just talk off the top of my head, I'm an interviewer's dream). So every person who has left me answerphone messages who are ummers, I've been keeping it on and having a good listen to it, to get the right intonation. Very expensive it is, on your mobile.

The story is fairly simple. Mervyn Peake actually discusses the characters and what they think. John Sessions, dear John, pointed that out to me and I thought, 'Well, that's useful, John, I really must read the books.' He pointed out Nannie Slagg's attitude to Dr Prunesquallor which was a help, you see. And I thought, 'You are a fool, you should have forced yourself to make time. You should have forgotten the bills and everybody else's demands and problems.' I saw John Sessions's script, covered in different-coloured ink, and I thought, 'Oh, June, you have become a lazy actress. I remember the day when you used to cover your script in writing.' I bought the books, and got a third of the way through *Titus Groan* but it's not bedtime reading, if you know what I mean. You really have to concentrate on this, and you don't really want to do that when you want to drop off to sleep. You want a nice detective novel.

June Brown has been Dot Cotton in *EastEnders* since 1985.

Andy Wilson: Nannie Slagg is just Nannie. She is the archetypal, iconic British nanny. She loves her wards; she grumbles the whole time; it is a very thankless task but it is informed by love, and that's it. Therefore she is a very sympathetic and attractive character. But she had to be part of the pantomime as well. There was the bit where Nannie is collapsing in the smoke-filled library and she is laid down by Prunesquallor to suck the air from under the door. We moved on and nobody remembered that June was there, so she just lay there. And we were doing another shot further down the hallway and this laughing started in the headphones. And I said, 'Who's that?' and it was June. 'What's the matter, June?' And she goes, 'I've just got it!', and I went, 'What?' She goes, 'We're play-acting! We are all play-acting! It's all silly, isn't it?' And she was right. It needed the gusto with which children launch themselves into fantasy games.

Chapter 7

Director's Cut

I first saw Andy Wilson hanging from the ceiling. On the same evening he had been run over by a motorbike and hit over the head with a scaffolding pole, and he was still laughing. It was the summer of 1988 in Edinburgh and I had wandered into a tent on the common next to where I was staying, and ended up buying a ticket for the circus. They were a young European troupe called Archaos working a kind of post-apocalyptic magic. There were the usual kinds of circus acts but with heavy electronic music and rock'n'roll lighting, punctuated by a mad group of clowns on motorbikes and in pick-ups who got into very serious urban trouble. At six foot four (tall for a clown or a director), Andy singled himself out and I laughed at him hanging from the ceiling of the tent playing a Christ-figure inviting derision. I can see him now.

It was several years after the night at the circus that we first met, and collaborated on two films. The first, *Dread Poet's Society* was about Byron, Shelley and assorted hangers-on meeting Benjamin Zephaniah on an Intercity 125 train. The second, *The Mushroom Picker*, was a three-part adaptation of a comic novel by Russian émigré, Zinovy Zinik, with a distinctly surreal flavour and costumes designed by Odile Dicks-Mireaux. *Gormenghast* was the third, and in between Andy had been to Hollywood and had won an award for directing Robbie Coltrane as the dry psychiatrist in *Cracker*.

Andy grew up in Essex, where, as he told Spike Milligan on the *Gormenghast* set, his first and decisive theatrical experience was the *Goon Show*. He would write out whole gags laboriously and act them out with all the voices on a reel-to-reel Grundig tape recorder. The family went to pantomimes at Joan Littlewood's Stratford East theatre, where he saw Spike Milligan play Ben Gunn in *Treasure Island* one year as well as

opposite: Christopher Lee as Flay.
'... a world of sunless alleys ...'
(*Gormenghast*: ch. 37)

'It is part of the disaster of the later twentieth century that there has been dumbing down in literature in the same way that people accuse films and TV of being dumbed down. The sort of sparkling poetic literature of the mid-century doesn't really exist any more and that's a shame. People seem unable to accept fantastical narratives as being of any importance, and I just don't understand that. *Gormenghast* should be on the shelves alongside some of the works of, say, Anthony Burgess, or Aldous Huxley. Too often it has been owned by a minority. It is certainly not a gothic horror, and anyone who says it is cannot have a sense of humour. You can't read the description of Flay walking down the corridor without laughing. It's a joke, a divine joke. You recognise him and yet he is funny. It's like Beckett in its wry irony, and it's like Buster Keaton. There was black humour there too – awful things happened.'
Andy Wilson

right: Jonathan Rhys Meyers with the director, Andy Wilson.

Storyboards for the 'Earling' ceremony.

'For the "Earling" on the lake, we had some rubber baby hands made because we figured that a baby of that age wouldn't be able to follow the instructions to pick up the ivy and the stone and throw it overboard. I have storyboarded it so you would just about get away with images of the child being held by the waist by the top half and moved across the raft, and his little hands chucking the ivy and the stone in were always meant to be rubber. You see his feet and you see his face and it looks as those he is walking but it's a trick. That's the fabulous thing about storyboarding. You know, it's magic and I like it for that reason; I like magic and the circus and pulling the wool over people's eyes. Film is all a trick. If you want a baby to look as though it is walking you simply shoot the baby's face and you shoot the baby's feet and have someone holding it either end out of vision. It is an alarmingly simple yet fabulous trick.'
Andy Wilson

Jimmy Edwards and Warren Mitchell. The *Goon Show* experience was followed by *Monty Python*, when he was allowed to stay up late to see the first series.

It was after *Monty Python* that Andy started making films, copying the Terry Gilliam cut-outs. He clipped hundreds of small figures out of magazines and pasted them up on the kitchen table. With his brother David (now an animation cameraman) operating a super 8 and an anglepoise for lighting they made endless stop action animation films. Matinees at Romford Odeon and films like *Dr Zhivago* gave him a taste for large and epic worlds, and he started to seek them out in books. He discovered the Arthurian myths, which he still thinks are among the best – perversely attracted to the central premise that all the stories are about mistakes, 'even the quest for the Holy Grail!' Early on he also read the collected Ian Fleming and Micky Spillane, liking the taut thriller plots, but now the bigger and fatter the book and the further away from Essex it was set, the better. Aged fifteen, he found *Gormenghast* in his brother's bedroom. It was about as far afield as he could get, yet still strangely familiar. A world that enriched him, he now says, and provided one of the foundation stones of his visual imagination.

Later, as a theatre student in Birmingham, he discovered the world of art, and particularly Max Ernst, a contemporary of Mervyn Peake. Ernst's cut-ups and collages reminded him of the Terry Gilliam images he had filmed as a boy. Andy's favourite picture remains Ernst's *Europe After the Rain*, a landscape of crystalline pillars with figures emerging out of them – combined images of decay and beauty. He was drawn to pictures from dream worlds and the life of the subconscious. Starting to work as a director, he discovered the Beckett plays, which he read as hilarious works of comedy. They reminded him of the taut dialogue in Micky Spillane thrillers which he had always found inexplicably funny, bald lines like 'She's dead.'

Andy left college set on becoming a film and television director and went into fringe theatre, where he was spotted by Archaos. One night he received a call from Pierrot Bidon, the Ringmaster. 'One of my clowns is broken,' he said. (Broken back, as it turned out.) Undeterred, Andy went on the next night as one of the famous Metal Clowns. There was always trouble with the Metal Clowns. They were set alight, dragged round by cars, hit with iron poles, hung up with their motor bikes and laughed at and generally survived only on the edge. Andy says that running away to the circus changed his life, 'as the circus has a habit of doing'. Pierrot ran the troupe on the basis that 'people want a good night out, that's all'. It was a very democratic style of performance, all good ideas were welcomed and included. Above all each performer learned to distract the attention of the audience to allow for a seamless flow of entertainment. All

Storyboards for the burning of the library.

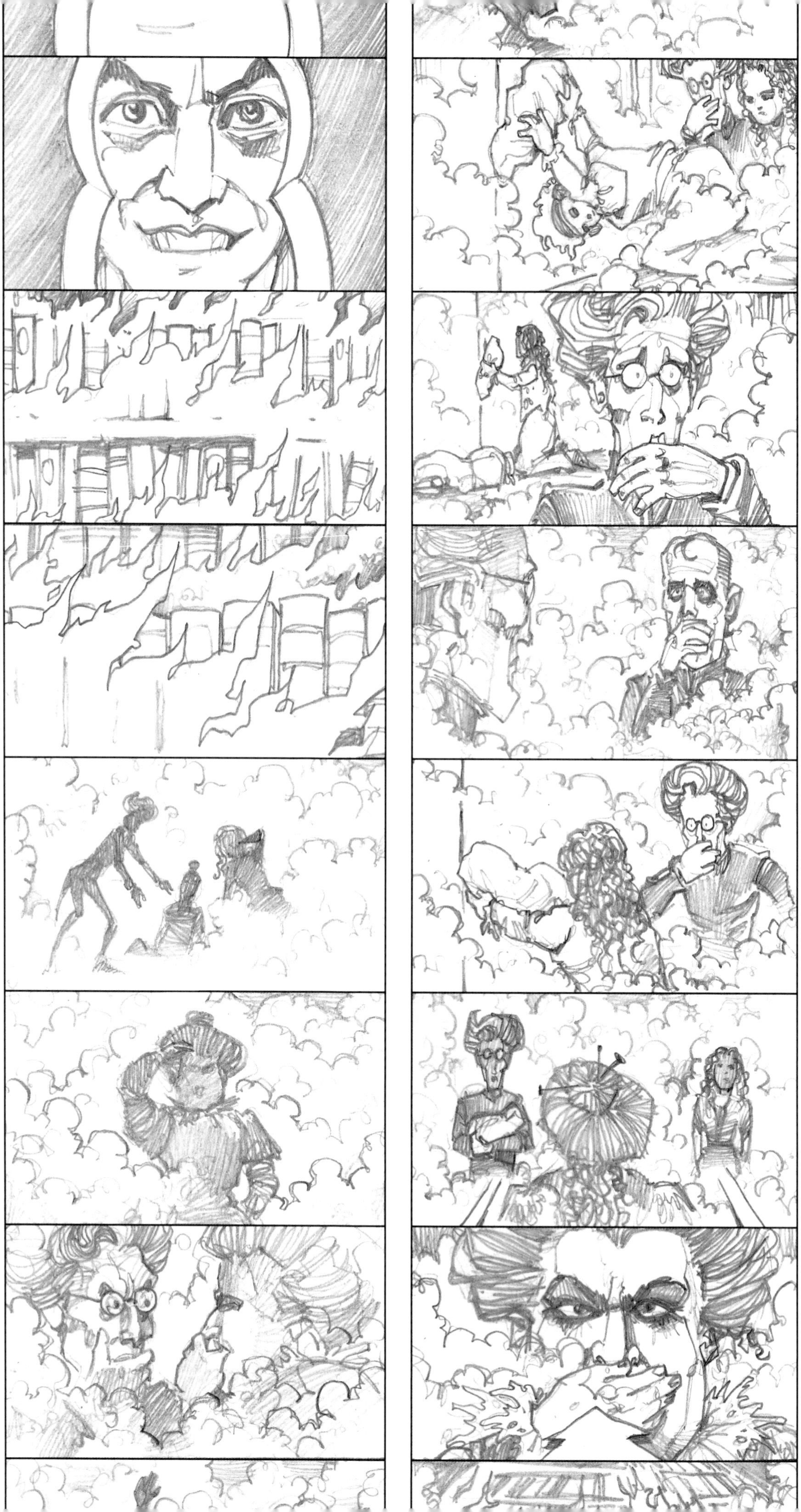

these are now hallmarks of Andy Wilson's work. The circus gave him his first break as a filmmaker when he made a short film about Archaos. Soon after that we came together to make our first film for the BBC.

The weeks before Christmas 1997 found Andy back at the kitchen table again, generating hundreds of little people. He has made himself something of a reputation in Hollywood for spectacularly conceived action sequences, and his storyboards for *Gormenghast* provided the central pillar for the development of the programme and the bible for how it was all to be realised. He drew round his Amex card to create endless windows, and filled them with little stick figures, showing how each sequence would be created, shot by shot. Andy's book of cartoons told us how much set to construct, where to put the camera, and what the actors were doing. Building on the comedy of Malcolm McKay's lines, he developed gags and physical comedy where it was suggested, and drew it all out like an animation. It was a book of instructions for the performing of magic tricks, the handbook for the Train Set. A storyboard artist drew up the final versions. They were dissected and broken down by the team, ending up on blackboards in the studio, and became the basis for the hundreds of questions Andy was bombarded with during the preparation. They are above all the living proof and the nuts and bolts explanation of How Andy Did It.

Burning the Library

As producer and director of Gormenghast, *it sometimes felt to Andy and I as if no day was ever quite straightforward. The schedule seemed to move relentlessly from one large set-piece to another. Every day we would arrive on set and gear ourselves up for another mammoth undertaking – fire, flood, swordfights, births, deaths, ceremonies on an epic scale, underwater sequences and so on. There were times when we shared a secret longing for a four wall set and a couple of actors having a chat over a cup of tea. The key to our survival and emerging in the cutting-room the next morning with the scene we needed lay in the storyboard. One of the largest set-pieces we tackled was the burning of the Gormenghast library, which involved a line-up of most of the stars, a lot of smoke and complicated special effects work.*

'The owls in the Tower of Flints seek their prey as heretofore and it is appropriate that his Lordship should, on the seventeenth day of an autumn month, bring forward the matter that is in his mind.'
(*Titus Groan*: 'The Burning')

Storyboards for the death of Barquentine.

Christopher Lee and Ian Richardson waiting to do twenty-second bursts of dialogue in the burning library.

Andy Wilson: In the Library sequence you had all eight principals, a real baby and a white bird supposedly locked into a burning building. I had to detail how the building catches fire from a little match struck outside which lights a cloth that Steerpike has laid all around the books. The sequence starts off with just smoke and then flame appears and than a conflagration appears. The flames were just gas burners which are distributed around the set, with hidden pipes and tubes. The smoke is this disgusting stuff called cracked oil, that is supposedly safe and non-carcinogenic, but is a hideous substance to breathe in. And after every take it clears away and you start again.

Obviously you can't do it in real time, and you can't burn or choke the actors. If you want really heavy thick smoke in front of the camera, the maximum that they can stay in there is about twenty seconds. So I had to look at the sequence from the point of view of building the visual impression of the fire taking hold on a very expensive set, behind very expensive principal actors and not kill them in the process! The trick I had to pull was to break it down into enough shots so that the special effects people in the background of each shot could start to build first the smoke, then a bit more smoke, then a bit of flame, then a bit more flame and then I could actually shoot simple lines of dialogue. I had to break it down virtually into individual lines, and I had to be sure that I was going to get the right dramatic impact for each line, while filming it in isolation. It appears that

the action is going on continuously, but in fact it is done in twenty-second bursts. It was pretty hairy. The actors sat outside having a coffee while the other people did their line, and then they would go in and do their own lines. It is a rapid cutting sequence so I just got away with that, and I couldn't use stunt people as you normally would for a fire, because you are close-up on all the actors all the time.

Death of Barquentine
The Gormenghast schedule was structured set by set so we didn't shoot the film in the order of the story. This meant that some of the biggest sequences happened across several days spread right across the shooting period.

Andy Wilson: Day One
We had to make a rubber Warren Mitchell head, which we put on a very old and very good stuntman who was about the same shape and size as Warren. They covered the mask with a sort of Evostick that catches fire really quickly, and he had a breathing tube in his mouth through the neck of the mask connected to an oxygen supply. He had to catch fire, run around the room, then grab another stuntman who was standing in for Steerpike, drag him to a high window and fall through it. We couldn't do that all in one shot because it was too long and the guy's head would have actually burned, so it was broken up into a series of shots. We filmed for a few seconds here, a few seconds there. The rubber head was flameproof, and we lit a new set of Evostick for each take.

Day Two
We had to shoot another view from outside, as the two men staggered and fell through the window, which was made of sugar glass and breakaway wood. This sort of thing can become very complex but, if everyone has a plan to follow and you know what the camera has to see at each individual second, then the danger is minimised. It was only two feet off the ground – and they fell straight into a bowl of water. They were instantly extinguished as soon as I got that shot of the window breaking. Then there is a vertiginous 300ft fall through the air from the top of the high tower where the window is and that was done with two little dummies (literally Action Men tied together with a bunch of burning rags) dropped from a model window sixty feet up. From a distance it looks like two burning bodies falling through the air.

Storyboards for the death of the Headmaster.

The cow was in in the field.

Day Three

The two stuntmen were set on fire again and thrown into the water, actually a flooded tank, then they went underwater to fight. I had to have an underwater cameraman, as well as a cameraman on top of the water, catching the surface action. So the underwater cameraman is waiting for these two guys to jump into the water and struggle, and he has got to get a shot of one of them floating away into the depths and the other one swimming free. Johnny insisted on doing part of this sequence himself.

Day Four

The final part of the sequence, in which the real Steerpike crawls out of the water to reveal that his face is hideously disfigured.

It was very complex shooting, with fire, underwater filming equipment, underwater lighting, loads of stuntmen, safety people, an ambulance, dummies, a tiny model window – the whole thing! You can't break that down from a script on the day. Somebody has to plan it with pictures. If I hadn't drawn it I would have been answering questions for about a week. There would have been people asking, 'When this happens, what happens then? What does the window look like?' With one drawing, or a sequence of drawings, you say, 'Look at the storyboard, that is what I want to see.'

Death of the Headmaster

As a film producer reading a script in the early stages, you know in your heart of hearts that some of the most cherished sequences devised by even the best writers will bite the dust early on as a result of the schedule, the budget or the sheer impossibility of achieving the effect on film. On Gormenghast *we made no such compromises. The sequence where the Headmaster sails through the classroom window in Episode Three was one that always seemed to me to be particularly ambitious, requiring substantial ingenuity and immaculate comedy timing.*

Andy Wilson: The establisher of the scene is the shot of the little boy swinging out from a side angle two hundred feet up above the ground out of the school room window and swinging on a branch of a tree that seems to grow out of the wall of the castle, doing a sort of flip in mid-air

Andy Wilson with the director of photography, Gavin Finney.

Design by Christopher Hobbs of the old headmaster De'ath in his wheelchair.

and back in through the window, then sliding down a greasy plank in front of the sleeping headmaster, hitting the wall at the other end of the room where all the other boys flick ink pellets at him.

This is a scene which is very carefully described in both the book and the script and what I had to do was to make sure that I could get the impression of vertigo, the boys swinging out on the tree and looking down on a courtyard. (You couldn't have little boys swinging out and back into a room with a real 200ft drop underneath them. And nor could you drop Spike Milligan out of a window.)

The first technical problem was that I needed a blue screen on the floor, and a blue screen on the side angle – so I could show the boys swinging out on the side angle to the tree and swinging out from the top angle to the tree. I also needed this greasy plank and I needed to know where to put the greasy plank. I needed to know where to put the door, so De'ath would come through in his wheelchair in relationship to the window, and that gave Chris the set design.

The little boy is a specialist gymnast which is another technical problem we had to sort out. I knew that I needed acrobatic boys to do it rather than ordinary boys. And also we needed to build and design the branch sticking out of the wall of

the set so that it behaved like a tree, had a little bit of spring but also had a trapeze bar hidden in it so that they could grab it, do their trick and swing back. You couldn't just simply stick a branch in the wall of the set. We had to brace the wall of the set with an enormous amount of iron work so that it didn't wobble. The ink pellets had to come from an air compressor gun, like a splat gun, that could be fired rapidly.

If my imaginings are correct then everybody will understand how the gag works. Whether or not I broke it down in a sufficiently Chaplinesque way to make it work as a gag is down to me.

Mollocks
Eric Sykes

Eric Sykes as Mollocks. *The door opened and the servant entered ... he deposited the bottle and the box upon the table and retired. There had been something sullen about his manner. The bottle had been placed on the table with perhaps too casual a movement. The door had clicked behind him with perhaps too sharp a report.* (*Titus Groan*: 'At the Prunesquallors')

It is such an enjoyable film. It is rather like an old actor's home because there is a part for everybody. From young Titus up to me, and I am getting on now. Well past forty. Let's be honest, well past fifty, or to put it another way, I am at the eight furlong marker.

Then there is Spike Milligan, who was acting as if in *The Goon Show* when he was in the wheelchair.

In my day, there were very few comics of note who were under forty. But now forty is considered to be quite old to be a comedian. People say it is the young man's genre. And that is wrong. Think of Jack Benny, and the fellow with the cigar, George Burns, who was funnier in his last ten years, until he was a hundred, than he ever was in his earlier life.

To be a good comedian, you don't learn it by rote or out of a book. The audience guide you. And the one thing that all the old comics had in common was vulnerability. No matter how tough they talked they were all vulnerable when they walked on that stage, and you knew it.

Nowadays, young comedians all look a bit fire-proof to me. They work on television where you can talk to a camera with your back to the audience, and then you dub the laughs on later.

I didn't know anything about this part until I came on the set. All I did before I came was to learn the words. They are recorded for me and I listen to them on cassette, and it is only when I've seen the set, and how everybody else is, and what kind of make-up I have on, that I know what kind of character I am. At first I thought he was just an old cringer, but then I realised that this cringer has a bit of a life to him. And now that I have been able to put some flesh on the bones, I believe in this character who has been with the family for ninety years. Before Prunesquallor, the John Sessions part, was even born I was there. And since I've come up from a boot boy, I am allowed a certain latitude.

The way I work is to look round the set and I

learn how to manipulate sets. They have chosen me because I do these certain things. I'm an awkward cuss and that is the beauty of my not quite knowing what day it is. But once I had seen this set and worked out what I wanted to do, then one of the tricks is that you have got to make it look spontaneous. Even if there are eight takes, in eight takes I do more or less exactly the same thing, so it doesn't throw anybody else. If you do something different than you have done before, then immediately the light goes out in the head of the fellow you are talking to.

And I had to work it out because I can't see that well. I can't see the expressions on people's faces. If I look directly at somebody they disappear altogether. It is like having a bush in foreground, out of focus.

I was a bit afraid of that goat, because being young its horns hadn't fully grown. If they are rounded like a ram, they can only bruise you. But those points were just about groin height for me from

the floor, so when he turned his head quickly, it was like having a marlin spike thrown at you, at the wrong part!

But the goat never took any notice of me. The goat was a bit arrogant. He must think that he is the best goat actor in the goat world.

Eric Sykes has starred on the stage, on radio, and been a key figure in British TV comedy since the beginning of television in the 1950s, particularly in his series with Hattie Jacques. His silent film *The Plank* is a classic.

Rottcodd
Windsor Davies

She realised how her first and only affair of the heart had been with a murderer. (Gormenghast: ch. 62)

Rottcodd. That's a name to conjure with. I see him as a sort of John Brown of Gormenghast! An ordinary man who is an old soldier and has got himself into a damn good situation with the royal family, so to speak. The trusted retainer for Lord and Lady Groan. He is an old military lad, who is in charge of the guards. I think he is a sort of honoured Captain of the Praetorian Guard as it were

like, if that is what it is. But this one got me.

What I like about the approach to *Gormenghast* is that we are not into magic and things like that. The story is everything. It is the story of a young man brought up in a very rigid society and feeling the need to spread his wings. That's the simplicity. But this society seems to be feeding on itself in a way. Who are

into the castle). And then he says, 'The east wing is eight foot under water. And it's still raining.'
In other words this is panic time for everybody, big trouble for the whole society. Not just some poor people caught in the storm. So there is a lot of event in it you know. It is a very dramatic piece. Life is relatively cheap downstairs and suddenly it gets upstairs as well.

– I suppose he is very near retirement. But when he leads the search of the castle for the rebel Steerpike at the end, he doesn't mess about. He'd kill you at the drop of a hat if you threatened his people.

There are all these little doorways, and it is a bit like working in the mines at times. I did some of that as well. But then again, you see these great interiors and you are never sure where they start and where they finish. I think that is part of the appeal of the book. It is time out of place, as it were.

I read *Titus Groan* more than twenty years ago, and it was odd. I got captured by the book, you know. I am not into fantasy, if you

the enemies? They come from within. It's fascinating, that's the thing that I like about it. And when Titus rides away, you wonder what is the other side of this divide. We are isolated as a rather large community with invented traditions.

And then there is this horrendous storm, like the myths, rumours and legends in all societies. But here it is a real storm! At one point Lady Groan says, 'What is your report?' And he says, 'The ground floor passageways on the north and south are impassable, the Carvers are quartered in the fourth hall' (because all these carvers, these people who are the artisans, have been moved due to the flood,

There is murder and mayhem in the offing!

Windsor Davies has played a sergeant for much of his long career, most notably in *It Ain't Half Hot Mum* in 1974. In the 1990s he moved up the ranks, playing a prime minister (Lloyd George), and a general (in *Vanity Fair*).

Swelter

Richard Griffiths

'... a huge shape arose. It sat beside the grindstone. It held in its hand what seemed, in proportion to its bulk, a small weapon, but which was in reality a two-handed cleaver ... his eyes were metallic and murderous, but the mouth hung open in a wide, fatuous smile.'
(*Titus Groan*: 'In a Lime-green Light')

Swelter was a monstrous figure – a monster like Idi Amin, who on the one hand was laughably comic and worthy of any derisory thing you could imagine, and on the other hand if you were in his hands and under his control, you could die any second. That is the conundrum, because you are laughing and you are invited to laugh. But please don't forget that this is Idi Amin, and if that cleaver connects, I am sorry, you will die.

And what is this, with all these little boys? That's absolutely not funny, but you have to see it in context. Swelter has an empire over which he has absolute control. Nobody is going to go down there. Flay is his exact opposite on the other side of the stairwell but Flay is with the Earl. Flay is a kind of embodiment of service. And the only person who could ever mimic and take the piss out of Flay is Swelter. It's demented, you know, it's juvenile.

But it is like the private joke that makes the audience jolt with laughter. Everybody has these private visions, they are all unique and most of us go around unable to express them in any way whatsoever – except usually with bad feeling and frustration. What artists do is just make it possible to see these other avenues in a very gentle passive way. And the best of them, like Peake, don't try and hit you over the head and hold a hand out for the cheque.

To anybody outside, just coming across it and reading it, it's immensely inaccessible at the start – all that stuff about the Bright Carvers. It took me about thirty years of not thinking about for it finally to sort of worm its way through my unconscious mind and unravel and reveal itself. But when I came to look at it again, I suddenly realised that the Bright Carvers were the world of artists. They live outside the castle, beneath the ground, living from the crumbs of the castle, only by the grace and favour of the castle. They all pour their lives and their spirits into the Bright Carvings, which are presented as gifts to the Earl once a year. The Earl selects one, and that Bright Carver is a superstar amongst the Bright Carvers. The rest of them trash their works and start again. Then way down in the second book, when Steerpike is being chased through one of these attics that are bigger than any of the warehouses in which they stored the Ark of the Covenant at the end of the *Raiders* movie – he bursts into this endless roof space and there are all these shrouded things. He rips off one of the shrouds and what is revealed are the Bright Carvings. What happens is that one is selected per year from all these thousands that are made, and as soon as it is selected, it is taken away, put in the attic, covered up and completely forgotten about. And that is the nature of art. That's what distressed Peake about it, it seems to me.

Richard Griffiths began life as an art student. Since he played Falstaff in a BBC Shakespeare production in 1982, he has never been out of work.

left: '*Silensh, my fairy boys ... come closer with your little creamy faces and I'll tell you who I am ... I am none other than Abiatha Swelter, which meansh, for you would not know, that I am the shymbol of both exchellence and plenty.*'
(*Titus Groan*: 'Swelter')

Chapter 8

Producer's Diary

opposite: *A score of bells and clocks had shouted ... from near and far the clappers in their tents of rusted iron clanged across Gormenghast. It was as though no mechanism on earth could strike or chain that ghost of time.* (*Gormenghast*: ch. 23)

below: 'It's a boy!'

15 March

The fifteenth day of the third month, and Titus, seventy-seventh Earl of Gormenghast, is to be born in time for the Millennium.

I get up before six, leaving three small boys asleep and set off for Shepperton in the pinkish light with ninety shooting days in front of me. Breakfast for the hundred-strong unit at Shepperton then on to S Stage to turn over at 8 a.m. with the birth of Titus Groan. The set is bustling. Warm red and cone shaped, it is

dripping with candle wax and bird droppings. Clusters of pigeons are being settled onto perches round the walls. Today we have birds, cats and a new-born baby. Nobody said it was going to be easy. A large camera crane has been pre-rigged for the opening shot of the film. The white bird, having skimmed the towers of Gormenghast, swoops down into Gertrude's bedroom and lands on the bed. The camera will swoop down over the bed as if from the bird's perspective.

We move with a following wind, and the actors appear on set for the first shot. Celia Imrie has been here since 4.45 a.m. for several hours of prosthetic make-up, hair and costume. John Sessions, dapper in his shock-headed grey wig and dandy heels, is given a case of murderous-looking surgical instruments to use. We select a purple freesia for his buttonhole, this will be continuity now and he will wear it in every shot. The baby arrives on set, the first Baby Titus, five days old. He is put in a small, warm cubicle with the unit nurse and his father and mother.

The unit is standing by and Andy calls the first 'action'. The camera swoops – and the crane jams. Baby Titus stirs and gurgles. *Gormenghast*, not yet started, grinds to a halt. It is several hours later that John Sessions is handed the small Earl, covered in stage blood and in full royal voice. He raises him over his head, 'It's a boy!'

16 March

I arrive on set to find pigeons still roosting in Gertrude's bedroom. Have they been there all night? A different Baby Titus as in today's scene he is older, the same menagerie of animals plus the white rook. I am yet to make acquaintance with the bird star although he has already spent some time with Celia. His portrait, wings spread, hangs in pride of place on Gertrude's wall. A typical Christopher Hobbs triumph of detail and economy – a picture of an angel picked up in a

*'There's seven of them.
One, two, three, four, five,
six, seven. Seven clouds.'*
(*Titus Groan*:
'Prunesquallor's Knee-cap')

junk shop, with the body painted out and
replaced with a rook attached to the original
angel wings by Christopher himself.

A cardboard box with holes punched in it
arrives on set, containing Jimmy White the albino
rook. Andy calls for silence and work stops on
the two other sets under construction on the
studio floor while we release the bird. Another
character born and one of quite astonishing
beauty. Steve, the bird trainer, lifts out a huge
white bird which flutters onto the floor of the set
and hops around surveying the unit and the
wailing Baby Titus quizzically, with its pink eyes.
It caws raucously like a storybook creature. We
set up for a take, as June Brown nurses the
inconsolable baby and Steve the animal trainer
encourages his bird to perch on the shoulder of
Celia's embroidered frock. I am reminded of
Steerpike's line as he surveys the Groan family:
'Mad, all mad!"

17 March

The scenes in Gertrude's bedroom are complete

and we move across to our main studio, K Stage,
to shoot in Fuchsia's apartments. Milk-floats with
'Gormenghast' on the front ply between the two
studios loaded with props and equipment. The
red set is immediately dismantled and work is
started to repaint and dress it as the blue cat
room which we will film next week.

Fuchsia's bedroom and attic are beautiful,
touches of the East, framed with the carved
doors and posts but carefully dressed with great
detail from the book. I spot the great 'writhing
root' on the floor. On the wall Christopher has
again with his own hand reproduced a number of
the paintings I remember. Two armies engaged in
battle, one in yellow and one in purple. A portrait
of the twenty-second Earl of Groan with tattoos
on his face, and children with a viper, in pink
and white muslin dresses. The walls are covered
in Peake-like graffiti and in one corner an original
Peake drawing lurks as a signature.

The Peake family visit the set. Clare, Mervyn's
only daughter, turns to be introduced to Neve
McIntosh, Fuchsia with long dark hair and the

'Soap for Greasepaint'

blood-red dress. She lets out a small cry and tells me that it's as if she's seeing something she's always known inside herself.

Johnny Rhys Meyers arrives on set for the first Steerpike scene. A coiled spring of latent energy. Before he can do any acting we pour green slime over his head, continuity from the scene which will come before this one, where Fuchsia empties a flower vase over his head. We're shooting set by set, so we'll do that scene tomorrow.

Steerpike and Fuchsia chase round the bedroom. He improvises, clowns and charms her, springing around the room with huge cat-like leaps, and breaking the bed on the first take.

The chemistry is electric and we know the seduction will work across the four-hour story.

18 March

The first death. Andy tells me the full corpse count will be thirteen. June Brown lurches across a shadowy vestibule and her tray crashes to the floor. Nannie Slagg's pink wrinkled stockings stiffen and Steerpike grins in the shadows. 'See it

as a gift from a kitchen boy, Nannie!' A sad end for Nannie but another thirteen weeks of filming for June Brown, who seems to have died before she has really started.

Ten feet away Christopher creates Fuchsia's attic of junk, where she will skip tomorrow. 'I am Fuchsia, I am me!' A vast cornucopia in the book, it is created on a corner of K Stage with minimal construction, a corridor between piled walls of Peakian paraphernalia. Christopher adjusts a giraffe head next to the doorway and places a cobwebbed harp in front of the camera position. The pigeons from the bedroom have roosting places amongst the piles of treasure.

26 March

Back on K Stage on the opposite side of the studio complex, shooting the cat room scenes. The cat room is being re-jigged as the christening marquee and a huge scenic backdrop is going up at one end of the studio. The vista is of the towers and turrets of Gormenghast and mountains beyond. Ron, the scenic painter, half

*'Been agaping, have you?
I'll fix you.'*
(*Titus Groan*: 'Fuchsia')

way up the studio wall, paints with enormous skill and speed. Christopher tells me he is the former head of BBC Scenic Design and has been brought out of retirement to do this job. Unassuming BBC boffin producing work of Hollywood studio quality.

Ian Richardson arrives on set in his Lord Groan royal dressing gown, printed with owl claws. He has been studying owl footage and is equipped with three pairs of owl eye contact lenses, the largest like saucers and which he can only keep in for minutes because of the discomfort. Discussions take place about the royal crown – does he wear it to breakfast?

29 March

We move on to G Stage for the Hall of Spiders sequence, a comedy sword fight between Richard Griffiths and Christopher Lee. We are now running three studios at Shepperton with sets being redressed and new ones being added on the other two stages. I arrive at the studios to find an ambulance outside, the normal precaution for stunt work and fights, but with the engine running and the backdoors open. Richard Griffiths, Swelter incarnate in his vast cook's overalls, is taking the air outside. He asks me if the engine could possibly be switched off as a precautionary measure, as he is more likely to die from the fumes than Christopher Lee's swordplay, even if it does mean arriving at hospital thirty seconds later.

Mid-afternoon I am called to the studio floor as Christopher Lee has had a fall. During the fight, he has lost his footing and fallen down a flight of steps. Filming only stops for minutes as Christopher, the consummate professional and extraordinary swordsman, has fallen with stunt precision and is on his feet pressing to continue.

31 March

The Great Kitchen. Early on set to get a look at the bevy of supporting artists who will inhabit this very particular castle kingdom. How will they cohere as a group? The vast area in the bowels of Gormenghast is one of Mervyn Peake's best loved and revered bits of descriptive writing, and is central to the piece, although we only go there once and remain in it for a short length of time. The place where Steerpike forms his world view.

The call sheet for the day reads:

    Grillers (4)
    Butchers (10)
    Kitchen apprentices (15)
    Legumiers (8)
    Poissoniers (8)
    Sauciers (8)
    Scrubbers (6)

We inspect the different groups, all dressed in faded striped trousers and yellowed white linen jackets, made from a consignment of old mailbags. Each category has a different physique, a different hat and a different type of facial hair – the butchers are to be hefty and bald. We weed

National Trust and not enough vast pagan chamber. It probably occupies less than a quarter of the studio, jostling with several other sets which must also have their space. On Christopher's original plan we needed seven studios and have had to make do with four.

But Christopher understands the magic involved in film-making, and Andy's tracking shot through the kitchen seems to suggest an endless heaving vista of toil. A fleeting glimpse, and a clever illusion which will linger in the memory. On 'action' the huge mouth of an oven springs into flame and the grillers stuff huge sides of meat into its jaws. Scaled up in size considerably and carved in polystyrene, the prototype is an Italian pizza oven reminiscent of a gargoyle. Up above the fireplace, a huge old bellows (a great find in the Gloucestershire warehouse) requires two-man operation. The Grey Scrubbers scour walls and steps; *legumiers* peel and scrape at mountains of greengrocery and butchers wield cleavers like some kind of charnel vision of hell. A second 'action' and Christopher Lee, bruised from yesterday but unstoppable, picks his way through the mayhem, the floor swilling with gristle, blood and rotting vegetables.

Warren Mitchell arrives from Australia and

Christopher Hobbs's oven for Gormenghast was inspired by the sixteenth-century Bomarzo Garden in Tuscany, where faces are carved into huge rocks.

The kitchen was filled with pastry-cooks, *poissoniers*, *rotiers*, *legumiers*, *sauciers* and Grey Scrubbers.

out more than we would have liked, as there are too many loutish Londoners and not enough pure Gormenghast. A lengthy delay before we can turn over as they still seem too pristine. A huge costume and make-up team move amongst the crowd smearing soot and dirt on bare faces and bald heads, spritzing them with sweat and drenching aprons in meat blood and gore.

Andy and I have been nurturing a secret anxiety that the set will be too small, a bit too

comes in to talk crutches and beards. He shows us how he will play Barquentine small and stooped over, spitting venomously up out of the corner of his mouth as if he's had a stroke. Lovely stuff.

13 April

Back onto S Stage to find the cat room is now the christening pavilion. The Gormenghast choristers arrive from the Temple choir and give us the first flavour of John Tavener's ritual music. They sing like angels, a piece he wrote for his father's funeral. They wear Gormenghast surplices in yellow ochre over regulation castle knickerbockers. The boys protest it all itches like hell and scratch between – and during – takes. They are accompanied by a dummy band of ancient instruments – the real sound will be recorded by the Academy of Ancient Music. There is a peculiar wind instrument made out of Christopher Hobbs's ashtray. The first prop he brought in, made at home one evening to give us a taste of the world. Someone else seems to be blowing some kind of carved duck. The centre piece of the band is a large instrument like a double bass. Christopher gleefully points out he has recycled the kitchen bellows, adding a carved head and a gold doily for fretwork under the strings. The sound is exquisite, at once ancient and searingly modern.

The choirboys are fascinated by the rubber Baby Titus used in the wide-shots. They finger it and squeeze it with a kind of macabre glee. Steve brings out Master Chalk – and he jumps on their arms and performs.

In a fug of sizzling lights, artificial sunlight beating through tent walls, the rubber baby blasphemously bounces to the floor and Master Chalk, now performing like a major star, flutters from Celia's shoulder. It is the first time for thousands of years the flow of the Gormenghast ritual has been threatened. This will intercut with Steerpike's climb towards power, up onto the roof of the kingdom. Unrest in the castle sets in.

'Who has done all this?' says Lady Groan.

15 April

Christopher has been up all night making jellies. He has designed a sumptuous visual banquet where the food owes much to twentieth-century sculpture, Miró & co. The crowning glory is a row of moss-green giant jellies in perfect geometric pyramids, each with an oscillating red cherry on top. The moulds have been specially made and every one, Christopher tells me, contains more than 150 packets of Rowntrees jelly. The entire Art Department are branded as doubters as they have deemed this an impossible feat, raising all kinds of problems such as the jellies dissolving under the lights. The detail Christopher is most proud of is the vibrating cherry. He explains how it is secured on a lever made out of a cocktail stick so minimal vibration at the base in the jelly, will cause large-scale turbulence once it is

'The matter of Gormenghast is the matter of the brain. It has wonderful things and terrifying things, great black holes and wonderful glowing horizons. I think it has to have all of those things in it and they are in the book. When Steerpike begins his climb out of the stench of the kitchen, he has this fight to come up through the stifling ivy and then he gets these great wide magical views of Gormenghast. As he sits there apparently basking in the beauty of it, there is a question over whether he is enjoying it or annotating it for future use. He comes down and describes to Fuchsia the great stone roofs. And there are wonderful descriptions of horses on lakes in the roof and things like that which alas I couldn't afford to do. We've done what we can but some elements are slightly beyond us!'
Christopher Hobbs

right: Mervyn Peake's seating plan for 'The Dark Breakfast'.

below: 'Hoot! Hoot! HOOT!'

opposite: Several generations of British comedy, clockwise from top left: Stephen Fry; Spike Milligan; Phil Cornwell; Mark Williams; Steve Pemberton; Gregor Fisher; James Dreyfus; Martin Clunes.
'There was a lot of mugging going on, putting each other off. Andy was encouraging it. He sat there going "More, more! Say things. Make things up!" It was fun. We did little rehearsal, and there was no respect. It just developed, like Wacky Races.'
James Dreyfus

transmitted up to the cherry.

I go to see Christopher later to let him know we have encountered a major design flaw in the jelly. At the climax of the scene Ian Richardson was called to leap on the table impersonating an owl and jump in the jellies as he flapped down the table to Baby Titus. To avoid the melting factor the construction of the jellies was so dense that he bounced off the top!

16 April

I prepare for a VIP visit. My three sons come to the studios. So this is Gormenghast! Where are the dungeons, and who is in them? They have come to see Gertrude command her army and James, age three, inspects the weaponry. It passes muster. Thomas, age ten, sits next to the director and gets to shout 'action'. I wonder if we really want a director in the family. They have rides on Titus's pony, draw castles on Barquentine's spare scrolls and are home in time for tea.

17 April

Spike Milligan, most senior member of the cast, arrives to play the Headmaster. Much has gone before him in terms of advice about his needs and desires. We are reliably told he may not be able to tolerate much in the way of make-up and would probably most appreciate being left in peace in his dressing room.

After arrival and a friendly exchange, we tactfully leave him to rest in his dressing room. He puts his head round the door of the make-up room some while later, asking indignantly why he hasn't been done yet. Surely he must have white death make-up! Once on set he tells me he has read the Trilogy three times at different points in his life and is delighted to be part of the film. Whenever I attempt to add something to an anecdote he says, 'Don't jump on my jokes!'

A slight delay in installing him in his lofty woven basket chair, as the wheels are a bit too mountain-bike and not enough Gormenghast. Gregor Fisher plays the Fly, a red faced puffing janitor of a character, whose main job is to push Spike in the chair and ultimately to his death.

We set up for the scene and Spike eagerly asks Andy for some direction. Andy tells him rather ruefully that his function in the scene is to sleep throughout. Distinguished snoring on the first take.

In the afternoon the pleasure is doubled as Windsor Davies and Sean Hughes join us. Sean is perfect in a cod William Shakespeare outfit. I remember Odile designed the first costumes for *Blackadder*. Windsor brings the archetypal Sergeant Major spirit to his barking command of the Gormenghast army.

The corridor of statues.

20 April

Stephen Fry on set, pockets full of carefully chosen props – half-sucked boiled sweets, snuff, pocket primers and catapults confiscated from his Gormenghast scholars. He sits in the Gormenghast schoolroom inscribing wonderful Gormenghastian geometry and geography on the blackboard. He is joined after lunch by his comrades-in-arms, Martin Clunes, Mark Williams, James Dreyfus, Phil Cornwell and Steve Pemberton. They sit in a cluster off set, capping each others jokes. Suddenly we're into comedy mode and the pace licks along sitcom style. We shoot the gags and the reactions and we're done.

Spike sits in his wheelchair and gives us great *Goon Show* voice. The moment to polish him off arrives and the gang thunder down the corridor. Gregor times a perfect prat fall on the greasy board – the gang behind him trample him under their feet and the Spike Milligan dummy, begowned and mortar-boarded, sails through the window.

26 April

Corridor of statues and Titus's room. This is the third use of Fuchsia's attic and we arrive in the morning to find a prince's room from a fairy story. Titus sleeps in a boat bed for a boy adventurer prefiguring the silver canoe chase at the end and his journeying in *Titus Alone*. Hanging over the bed is a Calder mobile. Another of the twentieth-century art references which Christopher peppers the world with. Titus lies in bed as Flay arrives to tell him 'it's time' – the beginning of the final journey.

The huge stone heads carved out of polystyrene flicker in the half light of oil lamps. Christopher was right in his decision to make heads not full statues. He argued that given the scale Andy and I have continually demanded, if he built statues we would never see more than the feet in shot! Titus, now grown, rides past on his pony, bowling over Stephen Fry, his schoolmaster. I am reminded of Mervyn's road to school and the giant stone statues lining the route. He rode on a donkey.

First VIP visit from Shepherd's Bush, Rupert Gavin, head of the BBC's commercial arm. I take him to the cutting room and show him the Birth of Titus. He laughs uproariously, and comments on how warm and vibrant the design is. 'I know you said it would be funny,' he says, 'but we never believed you.'

'We want our servants back and justice back and everything back.'
(*Titus Groan*: 'Inklings of Glory')

29 April

Eric Sykes in today for a wig fitting. Comes in with four gags prepared – a coat gag, a goat gag, a trampled servant gag, and a silly walk. He stands in the Shepperton carpark and demonstrates them in his courtly wig and a woolly cardigan amongst the skips. He'll use them all.

Bad hair day today as I contemplate the four 'making of' crews who want to film us filming – can't be done. Andy hits a low at 2.30 at the thought of the six scenes left today. I say – well at least the sandwiches aren't here yet. The sandwiches arrive on set at 4.30, a welcome break for the crew, but a moment of reckoning for director and producer when an impossible number of scenes have to be completed before the set is demolished overnight.

30 April

Andy tells me it's Lynsey Baxter's (Cora's) birthd͏ today. Flowers and cake are ordered and put ṇ her dressing room. Lynsey is perplexed. Right actress, right month, wrong day … Summer is announced, also early it seems, as the camera crew arrive on set in shorts. Christopher Hobbs now has his pushbike to get around the lot on – tells me he should have had it before but he needed to get his new reconditioned taxi to get it here … the last one exploded during preproduction. He bikes round the studios old-style, basket – the lot – and he's now gone into summer sandals so the season must be on the change. He skids to a halt at the prop shop, where six assistants paint book spines, moulded in rows of ten for the library. Animated discussion with Christopher about Trinity College Library, Dublin, as an inspiration and the discovery of van-loads of old wallpaper sample books which are going to make the whole thing possible on a grand scale. Out of the corner of my eye I watch a man sculpting a forest of petrified trees.

We ponder the key stills image for the show. Steerpike up on the Great Clock of Gormenghast, not swinging Harold Lloyd style as he does in the book, but straddling the hour and the minute hand – five to twelve. I remember watching Johnny's screen test with Michael Wearing, executive producer, and his comment – 'I always knew Steerpike would be the face of the future, whatever that is.' So here is Johnny Rhys Meyers on the eve of the Millennium with all the bravado and panache you could ever have hoped for, holding back time and whipping up the winds of change.

Only five minutes to the Millennium.

o tree ②

Vage section inserted
inting / model.

Certain style

Design by Christopher Hobbs of the twins' tree. *Steerpike had seen two figures walking ... it appeared that they were taking their lives in their hands as they trod that horizontal stem above a drop of several hundred feet ... Beneath them swam the pellucid volumes of the morning air.*
(*Titus Groan*: **'Near and Far'**)

Dr Prunesquallor's household.
John Sessions as Prunesquallor, Fiona Shaw as Irma, Jonathan Rhys Meyers as Steerpike, Eric Sykes as Mollocks, Niall the (wrong sex) goat.

1 May

Director's birthday. Another Marks and Spencer's birthday cake with balloons on. Those of us with children feel less than enthusiastic. One too many cakes from M&S over the years, but at least it's not the Chocolate Caterpillar. We do the photo shoot of the clock image. World War Three breaks out as the photographer, the two visual-effects supervisors and a committee of about six in all struggle with the science. There are several components – the actor, a large pair of iron hands way up above our heads, a blue screen, a white screen, a step ladder and a large pair of paper hands.

Over on the set the twins have arrived, thankfully before the sandwiches – Zoë and Lynsey in funny teeth doing synchronised greed, looking like two old dolls from a long forgotten cupboard. We smother them in a couple of sacks of dust. Over their bed is a big appliquéd rabbit, aunt-appropriate needlework, handmade as described in the book. Andy thinks it looks a bit Mothercare – can't say I agree, but Christopher Hobbs kindly tones it down a bit. Now it matches effortlessly with the Paul Klee style bird mural. First shot of the famous root room. The twins famously have a huge tree growing out of the side of their apartments. Next to their bedroom they have a room which contains the roots from the tree. Tangled and coloured to match the decor. We continue sequences from Steerpike's journey across the roofs of Gormenghast, and Johnny Rhys Meyers hauls himself up through a thick, tangled slope of ivy – wonderful part of the book. It reminds me of the best fairytale sequences, Jack climbing the Beanstalk or the Prince scaling the thorn hedge to Beauty's castle.

'What's it all for?' he says.

5 May

Meeting with the Peakes. They've come in force to discuss plans for a graphic novel. Fabian has allayed all worries about embarking on this one, by saying that Mervyn is big enough to withstand all comers. Then another with Alan Yentob to thank him for his support. I remember the ascent to his office a year before with Christopher bearing a large and intricate model driven from the East End in his taxi. The explanation of how it would all work and how we would cut this epic vision for BBC cloth was engaging and persuasive as Christopher mopped his brow with a large red handkerchief and swivelled round cardboard shapes on a sixpence. Passion for the piece and a vision of the world born in that moment which kept the BBC on track. Without Alan I wonder if it would have been made. Sebastian presents a gift of the Folio edition as a thank you.

Then dinner, and, as ever, Peake-style storytelling and the great generosity of spirit that characterises the family. They give us the sense that we are a group of creative artists bringing our art to their father's piece and that this can only give cause for celebration. It seems I am wearing the perfume which Maeve always wore. 'Arpège,' says Clare, 'she was well known for it.' Sebastian tells tales of smugglers and how they get caught by customs officers who can smell the fear on them. Then the one about the ship in the typhoon sailing for a month yet scarcely leaving the port as it's being blown back – that central recurring metaphor for Titus caught in the undercurrent of Gormenghast. Clare remembers how Mervyn had older twin sisters who died in China as babies, the first I have heard of this – 'What if we'd had twin maiden aunts!' Surely the Gormenghast twins …

6 May

Still hustling for a Gormenghast exhibition in the Dome ... can I persuade Christopher Hobbs to build yet another model? Matthew Bannister, Head of BBC Production, visits Shepperton, and we plot an afterlife for all things Gormenghast.

Twins on set. Steerpike comes to them in their dungeon and tells them the castle has been struck by the plague ... he orders them to crawl under the carpet. They dive under. Those of us huddled round the monitor have noticed the 'tame' rats, released for ambience, sniffing round the actresses' skirts and disappearing underneath – a terrible scream and Lynsey and Zoë emerge from the carpet with rats crawling under their dresses. The rats know when they're onto a good thing and repeat the performance on every take.

10 May

A grassy mound created in a tin shack at Shepperton, the smallest and humblest of our studios. The big scene between Titus and Gertrude – Countess tells young Earl what it is to be royal. Very 1999. Celia's prosthetic goes into meltdown as Gavin creates beating sunshine up in the reds. She sits on the mound side-saddle on a carthorse with a white bird on her shoulder and melting rubber on her face, doing one of the most difficult and most moving scenes in the film. Forever indebted to Celia Imrie.

11 May

First day on location – unit out to play. Breathing the air of Wimbledon Common and filming in Axel Munthe's house. A place of eccentric beauty – minimal dressing required for Gormenghast. The soothing routines of location filming – the trucks, the dining bus on the common, the actors bunked up in caravans, the members of the public who stop and ask if all these people are really necessary ... We do a make-up and costume test for Fiona Shaw as Irma. Odile has created a parrot dress and Fiona has an object like a flower vase pinned to the side of her head with flowers of coloured wire cascading out. No one is holding back ... Steerpike spends the afternoon fingering bottles of poison in the bathroom – done up as Prunesquallor's dispensary. A call from the cutting room to say that the rushes show a crack in Celia's rubber face in the close-ups yesterday. We'll need to remount the scene – horse, white rook etc. Look like being even more indebted to Celia Imrie.

12 May

Eric Sykes arrives and everyone is charmed. He is introduced to the goat, and I get the impression he has worked with worse. He does his first scene. Wonderful old decaying footman work, and as he sneezes a cloud of dust rises from his very bones. He enters with the goat, fighting it down the corridor. Why is he carrying a branch

'Long-necked Irma' partying in front of her own portrait, inspired by Mervyn Peake's drawings, painted by Christopher Hobbs.

under one arm? We get it as he carefully lowers it over the goat's nose to propel it along the corridor. Master clown. If Hattie Jacques had been alive she'd have been up for Gertrude.

We do photographs in the garden, between heavy downpours, of the Prunesquallors in Victorian grouping. Brother, sister, retainers Mollocks and Steerpike ... and family goat.

13 May
Long-necked Irma in front of her portrait. Christopher Hobbs, master painter, has done a portrait of Irma for her drawing room that is a combination of Mervyn Peake's Irma drawing and Fiona Shaw in costume and make-up. Fiona, in top comedy actress form, swoons at the sight of half-naked Steerpike, plans her party and longs for a man 'to keep clean'. She propels a paper knife into the ceiling, fuelling a wonderful piece of Sessions business where she brandishes the knife round his nose.

Clare arrives with astonishing family pictures – Mervyn in China with carvings, Miss Renouf of Sark with a bird on her shoulder, and more. She asks me to tell Eric Sykes he was one of her mother's favourite comedians ... I sit in a hallway

at the back, my 'office', trying to do business. Phone calls are punctuated by noises off in the shape of a bevy of small resident dogs who pass through regularly. Very small and very geriatric, there's one who always gets stuck on the same polished step and in time-honoured ritual has to be helped up. The residents seem very pleased with the goat, and it spends much time in the garden between scenes performing topiary on selected shrubs.

14 May
Night shoot. Tumultuous thunderstorm over London. It clears dramatically to reveal a still, perfect night as I drive down from north London to location, but a large black and purple cloud sits over Wimbledon. Very Gormenghast. Sit under large dripping umbrellas drinking soothing Heinz tomato soup with Stephen Fry and Fiona Shaw, who is wearing the parrot frock and the flower vase. They are waiting to declare love to each other. Location nurse unusually busy as one of the stand-ins falls in the fish pond, as they do in all the best diaries. Eventually we get the scene, snatching shots in the three-minute intervals between holiday flights into Heathrow.

'We want thrones!'
Zoë Wanamaker, as Clarice.

'The teachers are men who demand respect without earning it. They are all based apparently on Mervyn Peake's teachers, so it can't have been a very nice school, absolute hell actually!'
Martin Clunes

Sykes bombards them with gag ideas and orchestrates group timing. We love him. Fiona Shaw stuffs a specially made very expensive hot-water bottle down her dress as per script. We all muse on silicon implants and how nineties it all is. She finds a way of making the hot-water bottle pop out at the psychological moment. Poor Irma.

19 May
I introduce Sir Richard Rodney Bennett to the Peakes. Fabian reveals that Benjamin Britten started a Gormenghast opera with Mervyn Peake writing the libretto. There is a notebook with sketches and notes. We have dinner. Sebastian makes good speeches and Clare and Richard swap book titles on the back of a napkin.

24 May
Lord Groan's library.

We arrive back from location to find the library window where the family escapes is at ground level. Andy points out it will need to be higher if Steerpike is to rescue them by ladder. Design team go into impressive crisis management and the window moves miraculously up the wall by after lunch.

The set is astonishing. Row upon row of books. Twenty-foot high walls with bird's-eye camera positions up above, so the actors look like chess figures below. Half a pine forest around the set – sawn-off fir trees suspended with wire.

Lucky as we've run out of jokes (what's red and invisible? – no tomatoes). Irma gets her man.

17 May
Pay-off to goat. Eric Sykes brings in goat and it's the wrong sex. Exits riding it.

18 May
Irma's Party. The Comedy Zone sits out on the grass, eating the sandwiches and chewing the fat – Clunes, James Dreyfus, Mark Williams, Phil Cornwell and Steve Pemberton. There's a kind of braying noise they make when they're talking together, which we're encouraging. On set Eric

Warren Mitchell back from holiday. New, better babies, crying on cue as they must for this scene. Steerpike and Baby Titus eye to eye through the keyhole. The boy laughs, the baby cries. Zoë called at 5.15 a.m. for complicated twins make-up and is reported as having got out of the car, with the words, 'I'm too old, too tired and too talented to be called at this time!'

Discussion of trails for the programme and a suggestion to shoot a special trail in the cat room – I have to tell them we demolished the cat room set in March. It has since been used as the christening marquee before being demolished to make way for the library. Sets go up and down like dandelions.

Planning a formal royal portrait of the Groans next Wednesday. Snowdon and Lichfield say no. Too close to the real thing? For corgis read rook and cats. Get all the actors to agree to do it, then Make-up point out the whole family will all have been in the burning library in the morning, so their faces will be covered in soot.

25 May

Smouldering library ...

June Brown lets me know that the mother of the twins playing Baby Titus needs more help. June has been feeding them and 'nannying' them herself up in the dressing room.

Jack (photographer) puts his head round the door to say he can't get any pictures in the smoking library. Christopher Lee is wearing a BBC issue red smoke mask and Baby Titus is a rubber dummy.

26 May

Burning library. Cameras above pan the books. Party atmosphere amongst the actors, Andy sits behind the monitor doggedly working his way through smoking shots. 'It's a war zone in here,' he says. Christopher Lee, still weak-chested from illness earlier in the shoot, wears the red smoke mask between shots and celebrates his birthday. He and Ian Richardson are visited by their agent, Jean Diamond. She watches rushes and is surrounded by actors for the verdict – they won't watch themselves while it is being filmed. Christopher says he's been working for fifty-two years and can often tell on the first day the quality of the work. We get the thumbs up on the grounds of perfect casting.

The flames lick round the books. Christopher Hobbs has invented a fire engine. It's an Indian cart with a large barrel on the top and a hand pump. Andy tools up for a chain of buckets shot though the pine trees. I want to keep the fire engine for the exhibition but I tussle with Christopher who wants to sell back the Indian cart to offset his budget problems.

Celia Imrie returns from the death of her mother. Mine only dead in February just before we filmed, we had talked about her mother then, both knowing this could happen now.

We have shot Fuchsia's funeral without Celia. A double in a veil. The irony remains unspoken. This graveyard on Flay's grassy mound with Romanian-style painted posts for gravestones and flags, and a *Gone with the Wind* skyscape.

27 May

The Royal Family are still trapped in the library, God help them.

I watch Steerpike shatter the sugar glass through artificial flames and smoke, and realise how complex the sound design will have to be to make this into a real world.

We meet with BBC Worldwide to plan a Gormenghast banquet in Cannes in October. Do we still have the Miró jelly moulds from the royal breakfast? Should we serve green jelly with cherries on the top to International TV buyers in Cannes? Have I inhabited this mad world now for too long?

I go to Centre House for my annual BBC appraisal – a new experience, which includes my aspirations for the next year. We all realise I will be still working on *Gormenghast*. On to the V&A to discuss possible Peake exhibitions.

28 May

The King Lear scene. Groan and Fuchsia outside the burnt-out library pretending the fir cones are books. The last weeks have been marked by an anticipation of this scene. A full blooded and intensely moving performance from Ian Richardson. Andy uses the image of the picture of the brain geometrically divided – one section is the books, one the castle and so on, and they are being pulled out Rubic Cube-like, one by one. I see Peake's genius. The scene, brilliantly realised by Malcolm McKay, is about the madness induced by a life without poetic meaning. 'We

Jonathan Rhys Meyers jumps across a gap which will look like a chasm in the finished film.

should never have had the poets, their pen is the pulse, Fuchsia ...' Groan gives Fuchsia, the artist of the family, the kiss of death by giving her this knowledge. In gothic plate-sized brown lenses, 'I am the Death Owl.' He kisses her and holds her head, the seal of her suicide. The tears flow from Neve. 'I have no daughter,' says Ian. The blood-red dress, the girl raking the forest floor, swinging between love and despair, an intensely beautiful and passionate scene.

Nine Peake grandchildren arrive for their fittings. We have cast them all as supporting artists of one sort or another. They are reunited on the top deck of the dining bus and we eavesdrop on their differing takes on the whole thing. They come on set to watch Ian in the big scene. I worry about the distraction, still want them to see it. But Ian comes round between takes and entertains them with largesse. He seems in the greatest and richest of humours. The performance is assured – echoes of many of the Shakespearean characters he inhabits are combined and the ground feels very solid.

29 May

Rooftops. Steerpike surveys Gormenghast. The turning point. He sees the kingdom and sets out to climb by whatever means. 'I have seen the great pavement in the sky.' The devil on top of the world.

2 June

The Carvers Ceremony. The Grand Courtyard on K Stage – the largest set. The royal balcony with golden mosaic towers with Ben Hur scale. The Carvers enter the courtyard with their Bright Carvings. The ceremony described at the opening of the book – the carvings are judged, the winner gaining the right to walk the battlements on certain days of the month by moonlight, and his carving gathers the dust locked away in a dusty hall. The other carvings are burnt.

A towering set-piece – 160 extras including the Peake grandchildren, three cameras, Tavener music and Groan family, bird and baby aloft on the balcony, waving Buckingham Palace-style. The Gormenghast band hit large gongs and the flames lick over the bright carvings.

The carvers *en masse* – in our vision, a Mediterranean gypsy-looking tribe, in leather aprons and embossed leather sashes. We think it works – 160 extras individually dressed and made up. Wonderful attention to detail.

Shepperton hums with *Gormenghast*. Over in the stunt studio, Jonathan Rhys Meyers swings from the hands of the Great Clock against a blue screen, and jumps between the rooftops.

On the model stage, Mark Copeland has arrived with Gormenghast castle in his van. They (we think of the castle as a character it seems) have driven up the A12 from his Suffolk village, where he has been modelling in minute detail and painting in the garden shed. The roofs, towers and cupolas of Gormenghast in miniature, lovingly hand-crafted. Christopher scurries about between the three huge glass tanks in shirt sleeves, boffin-like, positioning cardboard cut-outs, playing with cotton wool clouds and talking to me animatedly about water temperatures, air bubbles and the properties of Dettol as a mist effect.

Alan Yentob visits the set. 'It's funny and terrifying at the same time,' he says. Relief that this comes through at this stage. We end the day with a Peake party – all the grandchildren in my office with Fabian, Sebastian and Clare, drinking white wine and listening to the younger generation talking about their grandfather. 'This is the best thing that's ever happened to our family,' says one, 'and the best thing that is likely to – except for weddings!'

This feels like the top of the mountain.

8 June

The carpark is jammed with horseboxes – we set up for the big riding scenes in the Grand Courtyard. Horses clatter through the studio as Titus says goodbye to Gertrude. Big trouble with Jimmy White who has been practising flying scenes in another studio for the opening sequence, where he will be superimposed over the turrets of Gormenghast, as he flies towards Gertrude's apartments. Every time we put him up on the balcony with Celia he swoops down and round the studio, showing off his new-found skills.

9 June

It's raining in the Grand Courtyard. Extras scurry about with Calcutta umbrellas and stars are stately under ornate Chinese parasols with rain machines full pelt. Camera crew trudge round in two inches of sludge. The studio is full of lakes of horse pee from yesterday and stinks. Gormenghast is grey and the mood has changed. People produce their treasured copies of the book. Nigel, the model cameraman, has a boxed set priced £1.90 inc. box, he won as a prize in an

Alan Yentob, Director of Television at the BBC, on set with Estelle Daniel, producer of *Gormenghast*.

The moment of truth for
Jimmy White, as he is
released 'into the wild'.

art competition twenty-five years ago. Keith, the
boom operator, has bought the new edition and
it is signed by every actor. Paul Tothill, the editor,
has three faded Penguins in the cutting room
acquired and devoured aged fifteen. 'When I
finished the last page of *Titus Alone*, I started at
page one of *Titus Groan* again.' We show the
cast and crew rushes and I ask the camera
operator what he thinks. 'I've seen it before,' he
says!

11 June
Monkey business. Steerpike brings Fuchsia to his
red boudoir to seduce her and to give her a pet
monkey. The monkey is a nightmare. It performs
to begin with but by the time the actors are
humming the monkey is bored. Even shooting it
simply, will the shots cut together? Karen, who
does continuity, scratches her head.

15 June
The rain has set in now in Gormenghast and we
start the tank work. We are attempting to create
the flooded kingdom in two studios. Matthew
Bannister is trying to get Chris Smith down.

Whoever said the BBC has lost its sense of
ambition?

Today we are on I Stage, where there is an
internal tank for filming sunk into the floor and
we have built one of the Gormenghast
apartments into the tank. Steerpike is hiding in
one of the rooms where the water level is half-
way up the walls. Slow progress in the murky
studio as we paddle round the puddled floor at
the edge of the tank and shoot Johnny canoeing
in and out wiping out Gertrude's army with his
catapult, in detailed action sequences.

17 June
The death of Steerpike. Titus, hanging by a foot
upside down in the tangled ivy, suspended by a
harness round his ankles by stuntmen. Steerpike,
fully clothed, up to his neck in the tank in the
studio floor. Both actors terribly uncomfortable,
face each other out for the last time. Johnny
heaves himself out between takes, shivering and
Andrew is cranked up and down for a rest from
bat hanging. Pain seems to inform the scene.
Steerpike sinks under the water and we see
Titus's face blur as the underwater camera pulls

'I wouldn't want to make it a children's film or to make it a uniquely adult film. You can make a dark weird adult horror version of anything. I could make a horror version of *Alice in Wonderland* if you wanted me to, but I don't think I'd ever want to do that because it wouldn't be *Alice in Wonderland* for me. Like *Alice in Wonderland*, *Gormenghast* has to be open for everybody at whatever interpretation level they are at. That is the power of the greatest story.'
Andy Wilson

down under the water. Titus fades in the eyes of the sinking Steerpike. 'You were lucky,' says Steerpike. The roll of the dice, the hand of fate, the inconsequence of privilege, fame and fortune. The central theme of great classic writing.

18 June

Most of the day taken up with an underwater camera sequence when the burning Steerpike and Barquentine fall together into the moat and fight down in the depths. Johnny and a grey-haired Barquentine double in heavy prosthetic make-up plunge repeatedly underwater, always seeming to stay thirty seconds longer than seems possible, as the underwater cameraman follows the double floating down to his screen death. Nothing comes easy in Gormenghast.

21 June

We leave Shepperton for a final burst of location shooting. As we go, K Stage, our main studio, is now being dismantled to make space for a vast fibreglass tank where we will film the final flood sequences and boat flotillas next week. We'd planned to shoot on the tank at Pinewood but it's in use by 007. The grand balcony, the big mobile towers and walls of Gormenghast that have been the constant throughout, are now being felled. There is much splintering wood and skips. Gives one a certain sense of anxiety watching a timeless and unchanging kingdom disintegrating to firewood. This is Peake not Chekhov.

We film at Claremont pleasure gardens in Esher in a week of scorching sunshine. Everyone relaxes just one notch as we emerge blinking into the light and put on sunblock and shorts. Only a notch, mind, as we face a huge crowd scene, a

baby on a raft in the lake, Jimmy White afloat, and much more.

Sebastian tells us the lake in Gormenghast is probably based on Arundel Castle. So will this do? Suddenly it's an English lake, not a created world in the studio. I ask where the dressing is for the lakeside that was going to give it a real Gormenghast feel. I am told the budget ran out and it's been cut. We find some bits and pieces from tomorrow's ceremonial scene to key in the world.

The lake has a natural grassed amphitheatre sloping down to the shore, perfect for our purposes – a huge crowd watching the Earling of Baby Titus on the lake. We've got a reasonable number of supporting artists but they will be duplicated in the computer. The setting seems perfect, but the sound is impossible as main roads thunder past and planes head for Heathrow at three to five minute intervals. Why is Britain's film industry based in west London underneath one of the heaviest flight paths anywhere, we ask ourselves. The sound picture will have to be recreated and dubbed on feature film style afterwards.

A clutch of European TV executives fly in for the day to watch the shoot. We do the scene where Steerpike swims across the lake and the twins wade out to meet him. How to explain the essence of Gormenghast to a Swede, a Dutchman, a Frenchman and a German? It's 80 degrees and they order steak and kidney pie cooked in Guinness in a pub with duckpond and cricket green outside. 'Mad, all mad.'

22 June

The last of the big Gormenghast rituals. Warren Mitchell regales us with jokes from a high platformed seat with a megaphone. The family are on rafts with 200 Carvers behind. Titus is 'Earled', to the tones of Tavener. Two musicians blow a fanfare on Tibetan prayer horns and we imagine the scene with the castle 'matted' on behind in the computer. The top of the amphitheatre gives us a perfect horizon line to superimpose the castle where today there is blue sky.

I realise Master Chalk will go out with Celia on the raft. Won't he finally fly away? Strange black swans tack across the lake, geese spiral overhead disturbed by our trespass and Steve, the birdman, tames the resident white doves. More bird magicking.

Gavin is not a happy man. He can't play God like he does in the studio. The sun shoots in and

out as clouds scud and every shot looks different. Actors are stuck on the lake on rafts, like a fancy-dress party on a pleasure steamer, as we wait for the sun to go in or out. It doesn't seem to be quite clear which would be best. Two hundred odd stand by in blazing heat while, Fuchsia-like, we gaze anxiously at the cloud patterns – stars, carvers, soldiers, spiritual ancients, frogmen, raftsmen, hornsmen, boatmen, boffins behind the camera, onlookers, picnickers, the whole motley crew.

Temple choirboys shoulder the ends of the massive horns – one is trying to hold his trousers up, they've split as he's been given the wrong pair – and the choirmaster lurks behind a tree trying to stay clear of the shot and conduct them in Tavener's Greek ritual music.

Frogmen cycle past in wet suits to reach the other end of the lake at speed. Stars idle about in the sun … Johnny Steerpike snoozes in the grass, Fiona Shaw and Celia Imrie thumb novels and the twins perfect their synchronistic interview technique with a bevy of journalists.

Gregory from the *Dallas News* arrives and I explain the world of Gormenghast for the good citizens of Texas.

Word from the V&A that they can't accommodate a Peake retrospective in the New Year, but why take no for an answer at this stage?

Rackets are twanging at Wimbledon but we only see the traffic en route to location – the TV in my caravan remains unused. Rain looks likely tomorrow and photographers for all kinds of different outlets are booked, unbooked and booked again.

23 June

Heatwave continues. The sunhats are out and we sit in a row of striped deckchairs, Margate style, filming stars on rafts. 'Seven clouds today,

Nannie!' Huge clouds race across the bright blue sky and the royal Groans sit on the rafts again for twenty minutes at a time between takes waiting for the sun. Celia Imrie sits in state with an incongruous pair of cool shades which she puts on between shots.

The final triumph for Master Chalk. It's time to put him on Celia's shoulder on the raft. Will he fly for freedom, drown or perform? Frogmen are positioned to scoop him out of the water. 'Will he float?' asks one of the actors. 'All dead birds float,' says Steve, the birdman. Steve puts him on Celia's shoulder and the hundred or so involved wait with baited breath … the sun goes in. Still he sits for fifteen minutes, great star that he is, then we get our shot.

I talk to journalists from Belgium and Australia. 'Is Titus Prince William?' they ask.

June Brown's last day. Goodbye and back to the laundrette. I remind her she was the first actress in my head and I'd always thought she'd play Nannie Slagg. I last worked with her on *EastEnders* in the Den and Angie days, when she first arrived as Ethel's friend, and we agree that Dot and Nannie have all the best jokes. The twins finish their final scene. 'Where have you been for the last fifteen years?' says Gertrude.

'Goodnight, sweet ladies!'

24 June

Today Baby Titus is a set of triplets, all costumed up so they can be swapped over when they flag or misbehave. Johnny Rhys Meyers clowns about between takes, dancing, pulling faces and entertaining the small brothers. The mother is concealed in a large hidey-hole at the back of the raft. The raft is pushed out and Baby George (or could it be James?), the only one of the three who can walk, puts to sea, surrounded by divers, crown on his head, with an expression of bemused interest on his little face. One of the several chilling moments when Steerpike and Titus eyeball each other, this time in the middle of a lake. Perfect performance from the baby even to the point of pushing himself to his feet and tottering towards the edge of the raft. His mother restrains a small cry as he flops off the edge onto a rubber crash mat and is scooped up by the stunt co-ordinator. Back on the bank, in the middle of all the excitement one of his brothers has taken his first steps. Just too late to perform them in *Gormenghast*.

26 June

We're in Honeysuckle Bottom near Guildford – a lovely old English wood with yew trees of astonishing age. Lots of horses and galloping scenes plus romance in the mist between Steerpike and Fuchsia. The Wild Girl sits up a tree and eats a live bird, a model wired up to move realistically.

27 June

High Rocks at Tunbridge Wells and a big stunt. Fuchsia slips down the rocks and Steerpike rescues her. I arrive to find Eunice, a feisty Liverpudlian stunt girl, all frocked up and ready to launch herself down a terrifying rock face. One of those low moments when you wonder why you're in the business and what it all means. Johnny Rhys Meyers has to follow her to the edge of the cliff and is harnessed to a nearby tree. Eunice steps forward to plunge – and the sun comes out. We wait twenty minutes and the sky gets bluer and bluer. We're doing a rain scene and we've already shot the first part in grey-skied drizzle. Finally the weather falls in, the rain machines start up and Eunice leaps off the cliff. We cut and the paramedics rush in to check she's in one piece. Eunice skips off her crash pad of boxes and demands a second go at it ...

Wonderful sexy chemistry between Fuchsia and Steerpike in this sequence. He tries to steal a kiss in the rain, but it isn't to be. Not ever. Even after so much murder and mayhem you could almost feel sorry for the boy.

28 June

Gormenghast-on-Sea. We take the stripy deckchairs back to the studio and put them up beside a huge tank occupying the entire studio, with towering castle walls built into it. Camera crew, assistant directors and God knows who else paddle about in waders and are a sight to behold. Rain machines full pelt and Titus skimming about in his silver canoe. Outside it rains too, all day. No play at Wimbledon.

Crisis meeting at lunchtime to discuss the final shot of the film to be done next week in Wales. Sunset and dawn for two options. Gavin has been studying the Ordnance Survey and has calculated that the valley we have chosen faces the wrong direction to shoot the setting sun. Christopher Hobbs and Alex, third AD, hit the M4 in the rain to tramp round in search of a solution.

29 June

Gertrude pursues Steerpike in the royal fleet. A flotilla of boats tacks across the tank, lanterns in the bows with Lady Groan in the prow of the leading boat, impassive. A close of play feeling sets in as we take the unit photograph. We try to organise it in the tank. I reserve a boat, but the idea fails to take off. We do it in the carpark with people in waders. Andy and I stand in the middle with the clapper board. The cameraman, first assistant and others have made themselves scarce and have to be fetched. Each time the photographer clicks, a key member of the crew appears on the horizon and is dragged in. Culminating with Harry the driver, who has to break into a trot to slide into the side of the photo, as the snapper finishes the roll.

'Can traitors live in air and feed on it? Can they chew the cloud? Or swallow the thunder or fill their bellies with lightning?'
(*Gormenghast*: ch. 70)

1 July

Four days left at Shepperton. Another day of frogmen basking in the tank. Some schoolboy splashing breaks out between shots – end of term atmosphere. Bits of set languish in the soggy skips and giant melting stone heads drip in the rain. Leprechauns in green felt loiter round Shepperton as another movie starts up ...

2 July

This morning we drowned Fuchsia. She lies on the surface of the tank in a fine muslin nightdress with weed in her hair. She is winched down from underneath and holds her breath, with frogmen poised below. Neve has chosen this day to invite her mother to watch the filming ...

Shortly before lunch there is a prophetic clap of thunder and rain falls like a desperate Gormenghast monsoon. The lights in my office go out, distant shouting breaks out and I gather that a section of ceiling has fallen under the weight of the rain – into Steerpike's dressing room! As the

And all the while the progress of the seasons, those great tides, enveloped and stained with their passing colours, chilled or warmed with their varying exhalations, the tracts of Gormenghast.
(*Gormenghast*: ch. 51)

fire alarm goes off I leave my office to find people exiting from the production office clutching papers and laptops. The swing door opens at the end of the corridor and a wave of rainwater curls down the corridor. I rush into my office and start grabbing production stills and various other unlikely objects and paddle to safety. Downstairs Fuchsia is well and truly dead and as luck would have it Johnny Rhys Meyers was not snoozing in his dressing room, so he's safe and dry. Maybe this will be the last laugh. I remember Sebastian's comment: 'If Dad had been alive he would have been sitting on the set clapping!'

We finish the schedule today and start the pick-ups. Children's party mood prevails – exhausted euphoria. I expect to find the production office wearing paper hats, like Christmas postmen in the sorting office on Christmas Eve.

6 July

Last day in the studios and we start with a boat procession across the tanks involving carver men, women and children, hens, sheep and a water buffalo. It all goes swimmingly. The last visitors arrive before lunch in the shape of a journalist from *Time Out* and three merchant bankers on a PR trip in awesome shades. We fiddle about matching odd close-ups and bird shots. *Radio Times* have succeeded in booking Lord Snowdon and he is across the way snapping romantic cover shots of Fuchsia and Steerpike. The mood is now one of a party past its best – when you know you should have left a couple of hours ago. I am the last in the echoing building, others

will return tomorrow to clear up for a week or so. I linger amongst the remains of chocolate cake and champagne and pack up my personals like a candidate for redundancy.

7 July

I take a train to Wales for the final shot. Paddington, Cardiff and then up the Valleys. I am met at Merthyr Tydfil by a local taxi. I ask if he knows how to get to our mountaintop location. 'Well, I know the way to the cattlegrid,' he says, 'but after that it's every man for himself. It's only sheep up there, you know.'

We rattle around for an hour or so, before finding the unit at an ancient standing stone with an enormous crane rigged, and vistas down the valley. They are in the company of Owen the local shepherd, who seems like a kind of Gormenghastian bard arrived mysteriously for the Epilogue.

This is the final shot of the film and we are to leave our Kingdom with a glimpse of something completely other. Andrew Robertson is required to smile for the first time. No great chocolate box sunset but the Seven Clouds lift and the light turns golden as the stunt double gallops hell for leather down the valley vaulting fences and Titus turns his back on Gormenghast. We've probably got it on the first take. Owen isn't optimistic about local weather for the dawn shot, but says it's unusual it's not raining. We know we've got a good shot from this evening, but resolve to have one more go at first light.

We snatch three hours sleep and leave at 3.30 to catch the dawn. Driving up the mountain the sky is clear and we are set for a fabulous shot. Two miles from the location we hit a pea-souper. Owen greets us. 'Lovely and clear an hour ago when I was up with the sheep. Be nearer lunchtime before this lifts.' We sit in the fog in the striped deckchairs, waiting for magic and dawn comes and goes. 'That's the way of it then,' says Owen, and joins us for breakfast in the bus.

That's a wrap.

9 July

Titus Groan, seventy-seventh Earl of Gormenghast, was born on the eighth day of the eighth month, and on the fifteenth of March 1999 at Shepperton studios, although he was already five days old. Mervyn Peake was born exactly eighty-eight years ago in China. Today is the ninth of July, his birthday. We have come down from the mountain and Gormenghast is in the can.

Prunesquallor

John Sessions

Prunesquallor is one of the most sympathetic characters in the book. He has a fatuous, idiotic, foolish manner, but that masks a kind person. He delights in language, which is why his language is so baroque. I think the strange little parlour quality to the Prunesquallors' house is quite deliberate. Gormenghast is built of vast, ossified, fructified

The Doctor with his hyena laugh and his bizarre and elegant body, his celluloid face. His main defects? The insufferable pitch of his voice; his maddening laughter and his affected gestures. His cardinal virtue? An undamaged brain.
(*Gormenghast*: ch. 2)

slabs of granite but amidst them, there is this odd little haven.

Prunesquallor isn't remotely given to change, and once evil is afoot, he is the means whereby evil is purged. The word prune both suggests cutting of roses and a purgation. He purges the place of squalor.

I do look pretty bizarre and my only problem with *Gormenghast* is that it is very hard to underplay. You've got to find a way of making a large performance real, which is quite tricky. It is one of the most overwritten books I

have ever read.

I thought of *Alice in Wonderland* in a lot of the scenes we do. But all the Prunesquallor scenes are like Dickens on crack (as all the schoolroom scenes are like Billy Bunter on crack!) There is something absolutely demoniac about them which takes them away from the cosiness of Dickens. The ostensible relationship between Irma and Prunesquallor is of

this strange sort of gothic Mary and Charles Lamb – living together like two broken comrades in arms. But the way that they stick the knives in each other, almost literally in the case of Irma with her flying paper knives, is very modern in an odd sort of way. They are caught in an awful hell not particularly of their own making, and they are having to get along as best they can.

I'm like the March Hare, in a very Wagnerian costume: with a smoking jacket and a certain chino-Victorian touch to the whole thing. The wig is a

cross between a Brillo pad and Bobby V, who was a marvellous singer from the early 1960s. It just plonks on like an old tea caddie, and it is glued on. The make-up is very basic, I slip in some teeth and I put some glasses on.

I do hope *Gormenghast* lays one ghost. There is this terrible polarisation at the BBC between period and contemporary, and they say: 'Oh, what they

want now are coaches driving up onto a gravel driveway' or 'Oh right, what they want now are people running around going "Get in the car."' I hope such an odd fish as *Gormenghast* will help frustrate such strategic polarisation. I remember a top executive at the BBC a few years ago following the success of *Middlemarch* saying, 'We now see that the British public want to see drama set in the early nineteenth century', which I think, with the greatest respect, missed the point. The point was, as with *Cracker*

which they happened to be liking just as much at exactly the same time, they just happened to be productions that had sufficiently realistic budgets. They were properly written and properly acted; and they weren't about chiropody in the Fens or something, running on for three thousand episodes.

Darling, when I am D-G ...

John Sessions is a leading comedy actor, whose work includes *Whose Line is it Anyway?*, *Stella Street* and *Tom Jones*.

Irma Prunesquallor

Fiona Shaw

Vain as a child; thin as a stork's leg, and, in her black glasses, as blind as an owl in daylight. She misses her footing on the social ladder at least three times a week, only to start climbing again, wiggling her pelvis the while. She clasps her dead, white hands beneath her chin in the high hope of hiding the flatness of her chest.
(*Gormenghast*: ch. 2)

Lucky you or I who are not Irma Prunesquallor all the time, but there is a bit of Irma Prunesquallor in everybody, I think. It is that person whose features are not enough to carry them entirely through a glorious life – turning back into frustration. I think that she behaves well in difficult circumstances, with a brother whose every second phrase is 'How ugly you are!' in some form

or another. The best thing that literature or films can do now is to be compassionate, and I really hope that this is. Before we filmed every scene I read the chapter of that scene. The detail is phenomenal, and there is a kind of innocence.

It is a strange place. I think the world of terror about missing those rituals is incredibly recognisable, and any sense about that being no longer the case is really naïve on our part. It is about how we are caught in them, whatever they are; whether they are Labour Party rituals or monarchical rituals.

There are billions of Irma Prunesquallors in the world. She is wronged. She is also incredibly clear. These characters are full of contradictions and moments of immense clarity like all of us, living lives of quiet desperation matched by blinding insights.

The energy needed to play Irma Prunesquallor just coming down the stairs is enormous. She is somebody living on the edge of her life, however small that life is. I admire that. This is somebody who hasn't given up. I think it is very moving to have people who are not of particularly great intellectual power but are not in any way stupid. The inner search for the great love or the prince who will come and take her away against all odds is fantastic – and it is of course what makes her succeed. The desire to have

a lover just about surmounts the wall of impossibility of ever getting one. She knocks over a few fences but she gets somebody. Successful people nowadays put ads in papers!

I gather Mervyn Peake was very fond of Irma. He certainly writes her very well. She is completely three-dimensional, even to the point of making a sound of squeaking bones. The structure on which the thing hangs, the actual bones, the skeleton of that personality is on a structure so taut that it may well make an actual noise. I know people like that, who are in profound second-by-second agony with their bodies, and unable to recognise that their bodies are in some way a reflection of their emotional lives. To make herself beautiful she pads herself out with a hot water bottle. People are driven emotionally to doing terrible things physically. But there is something much more innocent and much more sensible about using a hot water bottle than getting plastic implants put into your breasts which we do now. That's saved Irma Prunesquallor thousands of dollars. Who is madder – Irma Prunesquallor who puts them in for one night of enhancement, or these people in Hollywood, or wherever, with their implants?

Fiona Shaw is one of the foremost Shakespearean actresses of her generation. Her TV roles have included Richard in *Richard II*, and Hedda in *Hedda Gabler*.

Chapter 9

'Only Two Tunes'

There was still one question to answer. What did Gormenghast *sound* like?

Apart from the tantalising fragment of the libretto of Mervyn Peake's planned opera with Benjamin Britten, there are no clues at all. There is little hint in the books of any music amid the dry, loveless ritual of the stones, where the overwhelming sense from the sound described is the marking of time: **'The clocks and the bells stuttered, boomed and rang. They trod with their iron imprint. They beat with their ancient fists and shouted with archaic voices.'** (*Gormenghast*)

We knew that we needed two different composers. For the title music and the main music, I wanted Sir Richard Rodney Bennett, the most experienced film composer in the business, whose career spans nearly half of the century – he wrote a score for a Cary Grant movie when he was just twenty-two. But when we first contacted

him he seemed to be too heavily committed to other work.

While negotiations continued, we turned to John Tavener for four short pieces of choral music that would mark the rituals in the castle. His most famous recent piece of music was the closing cantata in the funeral for Diana, Princess of Wales. We wanted his profound understanding of Orthodox church traditions to bring a sense of the East into Gormenghast. For Fuchsia's burial, John Tavener gave us a piece written for the funeral of his own father. The pieces were arranged by Paul Goodwin, Associate Conductor of the Academy of Ancient Music, who had a double challenge. As well as scoring the work for each specific occasion, it needed to be played on instruments which *might* resemble the fantasy instruments of our house 'band'. Our group, with their bass made from bellows, a recorder from an

opposite: 'I did not read *Gormenghast* until I was in my forties or fifties. And when I did I boggled. It made me laugh occasionally, but mostly I boggled at it. How could he imagine a woman walking with a cloud of white pussy cats? I mean, the brain, the sheer audacity of the thinking of the writer. The wonderful power of words only really hit me when I read this the first time – to find that you could do with words what great people had done already with music.' Warren Mitchell as Barquentine.

right: 'The music doesn't have any real words, it is just vague sounds which we sing. It is just a kind of haunting mist of sound.' Tristan Sherliker, choirboy

The Temple Church Choir.

Hold fast
To the law
Of the last
Cold tome,
Where the earth
Of the truth
Lies thick
On the page.
And the loam
Of faith
In the ink
Long fled
From the drone
Of the nib
Flows on.
Till the last
Of the first
Depart,
And the least
Of the past
Is dust,
And the dust
Is lost.
Hold fast!
Gormenghast!

old ashtray, and a plywood fiddle, would always be there, with the castle choir alongside them. At its heart, Gormenghast is the simple story of a boy growing up. The choirboys who mark Titus's rites of passage are a reminder that the story is seen through the eyes of the young earl.

The Temple Choir, in the lawyers' church in Fleet Street, became the Gormenghast choir, and we gathered there on the last day of the summer term for the recording – the 'ancient musicians', with their plaintive cornetti, earthy sackbuts and original violins, and the men and boys of the choir mouthing a strange chorus. There was a set of huge gongs to provide the ceremonial sounds

of the East. A church has stood on this site since the twelfth century, so it seemed an appropriate enough place to mark the timeless eternity of Gormenghast.

By now Sir Richard Rodney Bennett had agreed to come on board. I had wanted him all along because of the way he could ground Gormenghast, earth it finally in England. And by a strange coincidence, before he agreed, a friend of mine turned up two Mervyn Peake nonsense poems with a hand-written score by Richard. The discovery strengthened my resolve, and I wrote him a letter saying what I believed to be true, that he was the only composer who could do it. By chance he received my letter, together with one from Sebastian Peake, on his birthday. He was moved to cancel a commission for Covent Garden to write for us instead. Richard wrote the title music to a poem which the teachers intone every night in the castle, which Mervyn Peake describes as 'an obscure chant of former days'. (*Gormenghast*)

For the rest of the score, Richard wanted to work from the finished film, getting his inspiration from what was on the screen, not what he may have read or seen in the studio. He came to Shepperton only once before he wrote the music. He told me that when he wrote the score for *Far from the Madding Crowd*, John Schlesinger had insisted that he should come down to watch them filming in Dorset, but he

The christening of Titus Groan.

The Academy of Ancient Music.

Sir Richard Rodney Bennett.

just 'sat there and sneezed and had no musical ideas at all'.

We sent him tapes of the completed films, and he sat in his New York apartment, wondering how to write it. Despite his long experience he admitted that the scale of *Gormenghast* was 'pretty scary'. A few days after receiving Episode One he sat in the dark in the middle of the night watching it, and he told me, 'Suddenly I saw how to do it.' Once he had cracked it, he wrote at prodigious speed, running up and down the spiral staircase from his studio on the upper floor to the TV down below, to check the cues. He said later that it was like reading a really good book – he just could not put it down. Even hearing him play it in New York on his upright piano, I could tell it was sublime – music of dreamlike quality which plumbed the undercurrents of the soul. And when it was recorded with all of the glory of the BBC Philharmonic, it was pure Richard Rodney Bennett, heir to the English symphonic tradition, drawing on harmonic changes from the Renaissance and turning them into music for the new Millennium. He thinks it is his best film score, perhaps among his best music of any type.

John Wilson, a conductor and an expert in light music, assisted Richard in orchestrating the work. It came off his fax machine in London, page by page from New York, and the sound of Gormenghast emerged. The music had titles like *Girls Afloat!*, *Good Morning, Slagg!* and *Breakfast Crazy*. But Richard said that there are really only two tunes in the score, one, a dark medieval tune, for the Groan family, and the other, a sinister five-note phrase, for the rebel Steerpike.

In giving a voice to Steerpike's malice, the

art of the composer in enriching the story-telling is distinctive. It brings a new element, not just amplifying the drama, but offering a different strand. Richard came to this conclusion independently, but it answered a crucial question. The full measure of Steerpike's calculating opportunism is examined in intricate detail in the books. But how could we get into his mind on film? We had discarded the idea of using a voice-over to explain his actions, so the music plays a crucial role. For example, when Fuchsia and Steerpike first meet, the scene is light and playful, as the kitchen boy entrances the Princess with his tales of 'pavements in the sky'. But there is a dark menacing undercurrent in the music, giving the scene depth and epic scale. Steerpike's sinister little tune reminds us that he is a trickster, a jester. On the surface, the story-telling is seen through the violet eyes of Titus, but this music subtly shifts the balance, so that Steerpike's iconic character is rounded out.

The score was recorded at the BBC in Manchester, with the full symphony orchestra requested by Richard, and John Harle conducting. For the BBC Philharmonic it was just another

session. One of the musicians wandered up to Sebastian, who had come up for the last act of his father's epic. Unconsciously echoing my son in the bookshop all those weeks before, the musician said, 'What's it all about then?' Sebastian began, 'Well, it's a long story ... '

And while the bass player rode his unicycle in the corridor in breaks, we checked that the computer had recorded the full sound the orchestra had made – the grand title music, the grotesque ballet choreographing the sword-fight between Swelter and Flay, the romantic drift of Fuchsia's mind, the sound of a room filled with a thousand cats, Irma Prunesquallor's hopes of love, the menace of Steerpike, the simple hope of a boy growing up, and the poignant accompaniment to the madness of Groan.

We had to abandon the studio during one session when the corridors of the BBC filled with acrid smoke from a fire. It took several fire engines to put it out before we could return. When we were interrupted, the music we were recording was the burning of the library. Coincidence? It must have been. As everyone knows, there's no magic in Gormenghast.

Afterword

Sebastian Peake

It has been said that the world of Gormenghast is timeless. It inhabits no epoch or period in history, and the characters both inside and outside the vast domain of the castle are as vibrant today as when they made their first appearance on the literary stage in *Titus Groan*. This is the Gormenghast trilogy's greatest strength, evidenced by the fact that fifty years after being written it is still being read by people of all ages and cultures.

Titus Groan was greeted at publication by varied but consistently enthusiastic reactions. 'It has not been written in obedience to any fashionable school. Mr Peake throws in all his forces of dream, vision and language,' wrote Charles Morgan in *The Sunday Times*. Elizabeth Bowen in the *Tatler*, who knew of my father, but as a draughtsman, noted: ' ... working now in words instead of line, poetry flows through his volcanic writing, lyricism is interknotted in the arabesques of his prose'. And Henry Reed in the *New Statesman*, alluding to *The Ancient Mariner*, wrote, 'I am forced to say that Mr Peake's novel holds me with a glittering eye. I have never so much enjoyed a novel sent to me for review ... it persuades you to read on ... gigantic set pieces of action ... magnificently thrilling.'

When *Gormenghast* was published, *The Times*'s literary correspondent noted that Mervyn Peake was ' ... a master of the macabre and a traveller through the deeper and darker chasms of the imagination'. *Punch's* unequivocal critique of the novel as ' ... the finest imaginary feat in the English novel since *Ulysses*' would have delighted my father. But it was the introduction to the novel by Anthony Burgess that put *Gormenghast* into the broadest historical and literary context, when he wrote that ' ... the book is closer to ancient pagan romance than to traditional British fiction. The doomed ritual lord, the emergent hero, the castle, the hall of retainers, the mountain, the lake, the twisted trees, the strange creatures, the violent knives,

the dark and the foreboding belong ... to a prehistoric England. And the magnificence of the language denotes an epic concept. It is uniquely brilliant ...'

The third part of the trilogy, *Titus Alone*, written after the onset of my father's serious and ultimately fatal illness, continues in a very different tone, although the atmospheric world already created in the first two novels is sustained by flights of the imagination equally as idiosyncratic, and are maintained as we follow Titus's journey of self-discovery.

Is it any wonder that film producers, who took up options on the making of Gormenghast from the mid-1970s onwards, found that one of the most problematic aspects of the enterprise was how to find the right 'voice' and setting? The recent explosion in the sophistication of special effects has coincided with the BBC's adaptation being able to make use of the latest technology. As with all the best effects, the viewer is unlikely to notice them, so imaginatively and creatively have the designers put together their vision of the castle and its inhabitants. Certainly, as someone always open to new ideas, my father would have applauded the sheer technical brilliance of these computer wizards. If he were alive today and could see his creation brought to life he would be highly delighted, I'm sure.

My father died in 1968. Despite the toll his illnesses took on my mother's own health, following many years of caring and nursing, she was determined to sustain and develop interest in his work after his death. She was the sole inheritor of his artistic estate and, taking advice from her agent, administered both the diverse aesthetic inheritance and made regular decisions on the many and varied new projects.

As an eclectic talent, my father's legacy was broad indeed. During his really productive years, roughly between the ages of eighteen and forty-eight, he had written three novels apart from the Gormenghast trilogy, had had collections of his short stories published, brought out five volumes of poetry, and produced over 200 oil paintings. These, apart from the estimated 10,000 drawings, sketches and illustrations he had produced during that time. He had also illustrated at various stages of his career many of the literary classics, and had written three stage plays. In the 1950s he was commissioned to write several scripts for the radio. A BBC radio talk he once gave, entitled 'The Craft of the Lead Pencil', became a classic audio treatise on the art and craft of the illustrator, the recording of which was sadly amongst those recently jettisoned from the archives.

With three teenage children still living at home, my mother was taking on a tall order, particularly given that she was an accomplished artist herself, a writer and illustrator who had continued working on her own commissions. But my mother's one fervent and recurring dream had always been to see *Gormenghast* made into a film. *Gormenghast*, she felt, *was* Mervyn Peake; was and is his whole world.

The first option for the making of *Gormenghast* was discussed as early as 1975, between the director of a small film production company and my mother. It seems hopelessly naïve to think that the idea of translating the world of Gormenghast from word to screen could ever have been anything other than incredibly difficult. Remaining faithful to the characterisation, painting appropriately and in believable colours the vast vistas observed by my father's imaginative eye, spreading its rarefied and singular patina over a thousand pages, must have seemed to that first film-maker as daunting a task as it was subsequently discovered to be by the other bravehearts who later took up the challenge.

As, over the years, various option periods lapsed, the difficulties involved in the making of Gormenghast became ever more clear. This did not seem to deter new disciples, however, and in 1980 the singer Sting was next to take out an option and try his chances. He had called his company Steerpike after the character he wanted to play in the film, and had even called his daughter Fuchsia. But even Sting was no more successful in raising the large sums involved, and, following several more years of attempting to finance the project, he retired from the scene.

A long fallow period followed, and although Gormenghast had been held as an option by one producer or another continuously ever since

1975, the two subsequent licence periods were taken out by two different American women. Both had travelled the world looking for backers, but there was a feeling about both of them – which proved correct – that they had taken on a task that lay beyond them.

Then in January 1994, enter BBC Television, whose sustained belief in the idea that it could be done was eventually vindicated by the energy, talent and sheer determination of those involved. The long journey towards fruition was to vacillate between the highs and lows of agony and ecstasy, sometimes reaching almost Wagnerian proportions. Despite the ever constant advice from our agents that nothing is ever for sure, and that caution is always advisable in case things go wrong, the BBC came up trumps. The go-ahead was given in autumn 1998, in a two-sentence letter to me from Mark Thompson, the then controller of BBC2. The saddest part of the whole story, of course, was that neither Mervyn or Maeve Peake had lived long enough to see Gormenghast brought to the screen.

From our first visit to the converted warehouse in Rotherhithe, where the extraordinarily exotic and imaginative costumes were being put together by a team of thirty dedicated professional dressmakers, to the vast film studios in Shepperton where the film was being shot, to the enthusiasm of the executive producer Michael Wearing, and the energy of the producer Estelle Daniel, the intimate knowledge of the books displayed by the director Andy Wilson, the whole enterprise was handled and run with a skill that inspired total confidence.

The sets, the stars, the extras, the boats, turrets, weapons and animals, everything was done on a wonderfully generous scale. The Peakes' hearts all thumped in unison every time we followed the action through Andy Wilson's monitor, as he directed and brought to life the castle, the action and all the inhabitants in a blaze of colour and dexterity.

Christopher Hobbs's vision and designs were stupendous; his ideas knew no limits. The actors, most of whom we spoke to on the set at one time or another, knew Gormenghast well, and were always so enthusiastic that it was almost embarrassing sometimes just keeping up with their energy and commitment.

Christopher Lee plays superbly as Flay, the outcast servant to the Earl of Groan, Ian Richardson the terrifyingly disturbed Earl himself, Stephen Fry is incomparable as the headmaster

Sebastian, Clare and Fabian at Shepperton.

Bellgrove and the Irish actor Jonathan Rhys Meyers takes menace to new levels in his portrayal of the evil Steerpike. John Sessions's Prunesquallor shows his breadth of understanding of the character, and makes us roar with laughter. The vast chef Swelter, played by Richard Griffiths, waddles and weaves through murderous assignations with death that chill the spine. Celia Imrie as Gertrude is wonderful, Neve McIntosh as Fuchsia lures us to her, with June Brown, Warren Mitchell, Zoë Wanamaker, Spike Milligan, Martin Clunes and many others

completing a line-up of world-class acting professionalism.

Bravo BBC! You have produced a *tour de force* in television drama that Mervyn Peake would have applauded from the rafters.

Chronology of the Life of Mervyn Peake

1911 (9 July) Born in Kuling, Kiang-Hsi Province, China.
For most of his childhood he lived in Tientsin (Tianjin), south-east of Peking.

1914–16 First visit to England.

1923 Moved from China to Wallington, Surrey. Attended Eltham School.

1929 Left Eltham, went briefly to Croydon School of Art.
(December) Joined Royal Academy Schools.

Mervyn Peake, with daughter Clare.

1931 Picture in Royal Academy exhibition.

1932 Designed costumes for *The Insect Play*.

1933 Moved to Sark.

1935 Moved back to London to teach at Westminster School of Art.

1936 Met Maeve Gilmore.

1937 (December) Married Maeve Gilmore at St James's, Spanish Place.

1938 First one-man exhibition, Calmann Gallery.

1939 First book *Captain Slaughterboard Drops Anchor* published.

1940 Moved to Sussex.
Began to write *Titus Groan*.
(January) Sebastian born.
Joined Royal Artillery.
Ride a Cock-Horse and other Nursery Rhymes published.

1942 (April) Fabian born.

1943 Left the Army.

1945 Visited Germany as war artist.

1946 ***Titus Groan* published.**
Family moved to Sark.

1949 (May) Clare born.
(October) Family move back to London.

1950 ***Gormenghast* published.**
The Glassblowers published.
Royal Society of Literature award.

1952 Moved to childhood home, 55 Woodcote Road, Wallington.

1956 Peake's adaptation of *Titus Groan* broadcast on BBC Radio.

1957 *The Wit to Woo* staged.

1959 ***Titus Alone* published.**

1968 (17 November) Died. The first line of one of his poems is on his gravestone: 'To live at all is miracle enough.'

References and Acknowledgements

I would particularly like to thank the following people: Andy Wilson, Malcolm McKay, Christopher Hobbs, Odile Dicks-Mireaux, Michael Wearing, Alan Yentob, Sir Richard Rodney Bennett and Carol Hodge. Thanks to the Cast and Crew of *Gormenghast*; also Mark Thompson, Jane Root, Rupert Gavin, Paul Lee, Hilary Salmon and all those at the BBC; and to the many colleagues and friends who have been involved along the way.

Special thanks for assistance with the book to Val Hudson, Eleanor Watmore, and Victoria Brooks, for her work on the pictures.

Personal thanks to Philip and Betty Daniel, who both died shortly before *Gormenghast* came to the screen. And, of course, to David Loyn, for his extraordinary support throughout this marathon.

Last, and most important, I will always be grateful to Mervyn Peake's three children, Sebastian Peake, Fabian Peake and Clare Penate. They have been generous in sharing their memories, and supporting the BBC throughout the production.

Estelle Daniel

A note on the text: old Chinese place names have been used throughout – the names used when Mervyn Peake was a child. His birthplace in the European hill-station Kuling, in Kiang-Hsi Province, is now Gulin, part of the larger resort town Lushan in Jiangxi Province, above the Yangste, now Chang Jiang River. After the birth, Peake's father left to go up river almost immediately to help victims of the fighting in what was then called Hankow, but has now been absorbed by the city of Wuhan. Peking is now universally known as Beijing.

Unless otherwise indicated, all references and quotes from Mervyn Peake's family, and members of the cast and crew, are from the author's own interviews.

Thanks to the Peake estate for permission to quote from Mervyn Peake's works. As well as the Gormenghast trilogy, quotations have been taken from: *Drawings*, Grey Walls Press Ltd, 1949; *The Glassblowers*, Eyre and Spottiswoode, 1950.

The following were useful sources of reference: Sebastian Peake, *A Child of Bliss*, Lennard Publishing, 1989, 2000; Maeve Gilmore, *A World Away*, Mandarin, 1970, 2000; Gordon Smith, *Mervyn Peake – A Personal Memoir*, Victor Gollancz, 1984; John Watney, *Mervyn Peake*, Michael Joseph, 1976; John Batchelor, *Mervyn Peake – A Biographical and Critical Exploration*, Duckworth, 1974; Michael Moorcock, *Architect of the Extraordinary*, Vector, 1960; the Mervyn Peake Society's *Peake Papers* – from an organisation dedicated to the extraordinary achievements of Mervyn Peake. Their address is: Mervyn Peake Society, 2 Mount Park Road, Ealing, London W5 2RP.

The author and publishers are grateful for permission to reproduce the following copyright material:

Letter from C.S. Lewis to Mervyn Peake by C.S. Lewis copyright © C.S. Lewis Pte. Ltd. Reprinted by permission (p.23).

Letter from Walter de la Mare to Mervyn Peake (pp.24–6). Extract reprinted courtesy of The Literary Trustees of Walter de la Mare, and the Society of Authors as their representative.

Letter from Graham Greene to Mervyn Peake © 2000 Verdant (p.28).

Letter from Graham Greene to Maeve Peake © 2000 Verdant (p.1).

Patterns for slips from Richard Shoreleyker, *A Scholehouse for the Needle*, 1632, courtesy of the Board of Trustees of the Victoria & Albert Museum (p.89).

Women with 'refajos', photograph by José Ortiz Echagüe from *España Tipos y Trajes* (1957) © DACS, 1999 (p.94).

Hats of Montehermoso, photograph by José Ortiz Echagüe from *España Tipos y Trajes* (1957) © DACS, 1999 (p.85).

Toreros, photograph by José Ortiz Echagüe from *España Tipos y Trajes* (1957) © DACS, 1999 (p.89).

Portrait of Elisabeth de Valois by Alonso Sanchez Coello, *c*.1560, oil on canvas. Kunshistorisches Museum, Vienna (photo: National Trust Photographic Library/John Hammond) (p.84).

Portrait of Queen Elizabeth I attributed to the 16th century English school. Hardwick Hall, Derbyshire (photo: National Trust Photographic Library/John Hammond) (p.78).

Ladakh – III, by Serbjeet Singh (1986), courtesy of the National Gallery of Modern Art, New Delhi (p.52).

The Petrified City, by Max Ernst (1935) © ADAGP, Paris and DACS, London 2000, courtesy of Manchester City Art Galleries (p.52).

Sark (p.34), *Girl Dying of Consumption, a Month After the Burning* (p.27), *The Baby Screams* (p.33) courtesy of Chris Beetles Ltd.

The unit photographer on *Gormenghast* was Jack English. Other photographers whose work has also been used in this book include Sven Arnstein, Giles Keyte, John Rogers, Joss Barratt, Tully Chaudry, Mark Harrison, Gary Moyes and Simon Buckley; Peter Clements provided technical assistance.

above: The Groans in full Royal Family mode. Jimmy White clung on despite the fan which was needed to stop Celia Imrie from melting under the lights.

Cast and Crew

GORMENGHAST
taken from *Titus Groan* and *Gormenghast*,
by Mervyn Peake

Screenplay by **Malcolm McKay**
Produced by **Estelle Daniel**
Directed by **Andy Wilson**

THE CAST (*in order of appearance*)

Lady Gertrude	**Celia Imrie**
Dr Prunesquallor	**John Sessions**
Barquentine	**Warren Mitchell**
Lord Groan	**Ian Richardson**
Fuchsia	**Neve McIntosh**
Nannie Slagg	**June Brown**
Flay	**Christopher Lee**
Swelter	**Richard Griffiths**
Steerpike	**Jonathan Rhys Meyers**
Clarice	**Zoë Wanamaker**
Cora	**Lynsey Baxter**
Irma Prunesquallor	**Fiona Shaw**
Bookman	**George Yiasoumi**
Keda	**Olga Sosnovska**
Mollocks	**Eric Sykes**
Poet	**Sean Hughes**
Rottcodd	**Windsor Davies**
Titus	**Cameron Powrie**
	Andrew Robertson
Professor Bellgove	**Stephen Fry**
Professor Perch	**Mark Williams**
Professor Fluke	**James Dreyfus**
Professor Shred	**Phil Cornwell**
Professor Mule	**Steve Pemberton**
Professor Flower	**Martin Clunes**
De'ath	**Spike Milligan**
The Fly	**Gregor Fisher**
Doggit	**Lewis Rose**
Boatman	**Tim Barlow**
Wild Girl	**Caroline Nelson**
	Daniela Zocchi

THE CREW

Production Manager	**David Mason**
Location Manager	**Peter Tullo**
Script Supervisor	**Karen Jones**
Second Assistant Director	**Giles Butler**
Third Assistant Director	**Alex Gibb**
Floor Runner	**Nicholas Hopkins**
Production Executive	**Howard Kingston**
Production Co-ordinator	**Phyl Allarie**
Production Accountant	**Sarah Fisher**
Assistant Production Accountant	**Peter Eardley**
Assistant to the Producer	**Ashley Russell**
Producer's Secretary	**Eleanor Watmore**
Production Runner	**Chris Dall**
Camera Operator	**Mike Proudfoot**
Focus Puller	**Simon Finney**
Clapper Loader	**Rod Marley**
Camera Grip	**Tony Turner**
Crane Grip	**Dick Lee**
Gaffer	**Terry Hunt**
Best Boy	**Richard Potter**
Camera Trainee	**Pip Hare**
Electricians	**Phil Penfold**
	Dick Conway
	Tommy Brown
	Graham Driscoll
Rigging Gaffer	**Tony Hannington**
Standby Rigger	**Robert Diebelius**

Senior Art Director	**Andrew Munro**
Art Director	**David Hindle**
Assistant Art Directors	**Ben Smith**
	Tom Wales
Art Department Assistants	**Ben Munro**
	Jenny Edwards
Art Department Runner	**Zoë Smith**
Scenic Artist	**Ron King**
Model-maker	**Mark Copeland**
Storyboard Artist	**Paul Garner**
Graphic Design	**Christine Büttner**
Production Buyer	**Trisha Edwards**
Construction Manager	**Alan Chesters**
Supervising Carpenter	**Ned Kelly**
Property Master	**Ray Perry**
Standby Props	**Wesley Peppiatt**
	Joshua Critcher
Storeman	**Paul Bradburn**
Dressing Props	**Danny Evans**
	Ian Young
Standby Carpenter	**Steve Rogers**
Standby Painter	**Robert Betts**
Standby Stagehand	**Terry Meadows**
Costume Design Assistants	**Marion Weise**
	Carin Hoff
Wardrobe Assistants	**Samantha Mealing**
	Sara Meek
	Barbara Harrington
Make-up Artists	**Sandra Shepherd**
	Diane Chenery-Wickens
	Julie Dartnell
Hairdresser	**Liz Michie**
Prosthetics Make-up	**David White**
Second Unit Director	**Matthew Cope**
Model Unit Camera	**Nigel Stone**
Special Effects	**Tom Harris**
Visual Effects Supervisor	**Simon Giles**
Stunt Co-ordinator	**Andy Bradford**
Animal Consultants	**Steve Harty**
	Sue Clark
Movement Coach	**Hilary Westlake**
Swordmaster	**Richard Bonehill**
Sound Recordist	**Alistair Crocker**
Boom Operator	**Keith Batten**
Dubbing Mixer	**Paul Carr**
Dubbing Editors	**Lee Critchlow**
	Jon Hemming
	Mike Redfern
Assembly Editor	**Mark Gravil**
Assistant Film Editor	**Angela Bailey**
Voice Coach	**Andrew Jack**
Casting Director	**Marilyn Johnson**
Script Editor	**Mark Sparrow**

Music composed by **Richard Rodney Bennett**.
Played by the BBC Philharmonic, conducted by **John Harle**.
Assistant to the composer was **John Wilson**.

Choral Music by **John Tavener**, played by the **Academy of Ancient Music**, conducted by **Paul Goodwin**, with the **Temple Church Choir** directed by **Stephen Layton**.

Line Producer	**Al Burgess**
Make-up Designers	**Joan Hills**
	Christine Greenwood
Film Editor	**Paul Tothill**
Director of Photography	**Gavin Finney**
Costume Designer	**Odile Dicks-Mireaux**
Production Designer	**Christopher Hobbs**
Executive Producers	**Michael Wearing**
	Hilary Salmon